M000235986

—RETHiNK®—
remoting

Take **Remote Control** of
YOUR LIFE

PAUL O'MAHONY & **JOHNNY BEIRNE**

All rights reserved. No part of this publication may be reproduced, stored in a retrieval system, or transmitted, in any form or by any means, electronic, photocopying, recording, or otherwise, without the prior written permission.

Copyright © 2021 by Paul O'Mahony and Johnny Beirne

—RETHiNK®—
remoting

PAUL O'MAHONY & **JOHNNY BEIRNE**

Contents

Foreword

The world of work has changed, and quite simply is never going back to the "way things were". For most people, when they chose their current home to live and sleep in - and possibly to raise their family in - little did they think it would also become the office that they are expected to work from!

Regardless of our personal opinions on the global shift of work from the office block to the kitchen table, resistance is futile!

Remote working is here to stay.

However, working from home (whether for yourself or for an employer) does not have to be as daunting as we may all have felt it was, initially. Working from home or "remoting" as it's becoming commonly known brings opportunities that most are not even aware of.

It presents an opportunity to redefine what "living" means in the 21st century and to rethink our goals, plans and expectations from our life and career. It can become an incredibly powerful stimulus, reigniting a spark that may have long-since been extinguished by the banality of the day-to-day routine.

I first met Johnny Beirne over a decade ago when I was a participant in one of his workshops. He was a man ahead of his time, already selling others on the idea of generating an income without physical boundaries. I was impressed by his knowledge of building businesses and careers through the internet, so we connected and have remained in touch ever since.

When he reached out to me with the idea that the world was now ready for what he had been building for over a decade, I jumped at the opportunity to be involved. I totally agreed that whether people like it or not, the time has come to take remote control of their lives. Through this book, we want to share the easiest, most efficient and affordable way of doing exactly this.

Congratulations on picking up this book. My advice to you now would be to digest what you read and put it into action immediately, in order to get a huge head-start over the rest of society. While most are resistant to change, those who embrace it will end up being so far ahead that they will soon forget about the "way things were". Instead they will wonder why they ever wished to revisit the past when the future looked so rosy! Enjoy the shift!

Paul O'Mahony

Founder of RETHiNK Academy Ltd, FUNancial Freedom Ltd and 16-time USA Today & Wall Street Journal Bestselling Author, Speaker & Serial Entrepreneur (and long-time digital remoter!)

Introduction

Assuming that we sleep for 7 or 8 hours each night, work accounts for nearly half our waking hours. For many, work dominates more than half of their lives.

Work doesn't just dictate what we do with our time and how much money we receive in return for our efforts – it dictates our standard of living and determines what we are able to do when we aren't working. It determines who we spend much of our time with, and the environment within which we spend it.

Our working day could easily be extended by 2 or 3 hours (or more) when we add the time spent (or should that be, lost) commuting to and from the office.

This is where remote working starts to seem like an obvious and logical solution to the problems of wasted time. It presents us with an opportunity to improve the quality of existence immeasurably, by taking back the remote control of our life.

Remote working is not a new innovation. Telecommuting has been around since the seventies, and many people in diverse careers have successfully worked remotely, either at home or on the road for many years.

The global pandemic of 2020 coincided with momentous advances in technology and made this way of working more commonplace and much more widely accepted. Over 1.25 billion 'knowledge workers' have spent much of 2020 and 2021 working from home. Indications suggest that things will remain that way for the long term, or at least not return to the way they were pre-pandemic.

People all over the world have recognised that the remote revolution offers a new way of life and promises a new-found freedom to those who embrace it.

■ Time is our most valuable resource

One of the biggest revelations for many, has been the effects of remote working on the benefit they get from their time.

- They're no longer wasting hours each day commuting and are able to start (and finish) work earlier or later depending on their preferences

- They're free to spend more time with their loved ones, eating meals together that may have otherwise been missed

- They're able to fit in exercise, hobbies and social commitments around their working day with more time available to use in ways that enrich their life

- They've used the time that was previously wasted, starting side-businesses or learning new skills.

Employees and entrepreneurs alike have demonstrated that productivity and success aren't reliant on being physically present in a formal place of business. After initially having to adapt, many businesses and the people working within them have gone on to thrive and succeed. Remote working has been at the heart of those successes.

This time saving and the shift in working methods present a massive opportunity for people to rethink how and where they work, and who they work for. It has provided a real opportunity for regular people to reinvent, recalibrate and reshape their lives.

While organisations are helping their employees to adopt and adapt to this new way of working, entrepreneurs and business owners are left to figure it all out for themselves.

At the same time, as more people become used to working remotely doing jobs that were previously office-based, many are beginning to wonder *"could I work remotely, for myself?"*

Could they change their situation from being a good employee, instead becoming a good employer and working for themselves as their own boss?

That's where we can help.

■ RETHiNK Remoting

Hello, and welcome to RETHiNK Remoting – your guide to the remote working revolution.

We are Paul O'Mahony and Johnny Beirne and we're pleased to bring you our collective knowledge and experience of remote working and entrepreneurship, within the pages of this book.

Our aim is to help you to recognise the massive potential offered by remote working (or remoting as we call it). We want to help you understand how you can embrace it in your own working life, to realise the enormously beneficial effects that it can unlock.

■ The rise of remoting

More people than ever are working online from home or from a nearby co-working space and it looks like remoting is here to stay.

It used to be that remote working or working from home was treated with disdain. The assumption was that those who chose to work remotely were slacking-off, watching daytime TV and eating endless bowls of cereal in their pyjamas while keeping a cursory eye on their email inbox and their phone to hand in case their boss tried to contact them.

Many employers were cautious about allowing remote working. Some would require staff to document what they were planning on doing in the coming day before agreeing to it. They'd check-up the day after, to make sure the work had been done – like teachers checking their pupils' homework.

The misguided and false assumption was that if you were present in the office and within sight, your time could be accounted for and your efforts would be focused. If you were working at home, you needed to be micro-managed and your activities needed to be monitored to ensure productivity.

Nowadays, employers understand that a bit of flexibility and trust extended to their workforce will yield good-will and dedication in return. Equipping staff with the technology and the trust to work from home seems like a good way of doing this, at little marginal cost and with enormous potential returns.

Many employers now only provide desk-space for the equivalent of 80% of their workforce or less, on the assumption that the remainder will work from home for at least some of the time. This yields financial savings for businesses too, which in turn allows them to reinvest in technology and flexible working solutions that give workers even more choice over how, when and where they work.

This was all becoming the norm even before the pandemic struck in late 2019, forcing office workers all over the world to adapt rapidly to remote working.

■ The Remoting Revolution

Since then, many businesses have recognised that there isn't a need or obvious benefit in maintaining office space for all employees. There's also not a need to drag employees into work in order to guarantee productivity. Businesses continued to remain profitable in spite of the forced change of circumstances. Employees in turn realised they could work just as effectively from home, with a little support and the right tools and technologies.

People all over the world have recognised that the remote revolution offers a new way of life and promises a new-found, and much sought-after freedom for those who embrace it. The remote revolution is an enabler for them to reinvent themselves; to rethink how they live, how they work, where they work and indeed who they work for.

Many have had a remote revelation, realising *"hey, if I can work from home for someone else, maybe I can do it for myself?"*

They are using this new-normal to set up their own online businesses – as a means of moving from being a great employee to instead be their own employer; to evolve from having a boss to being a boss for themselves.

It's a chance to work at their **own pace** from their **own place**.

Through the chapters of this book we will demonstrate how you too can benefit from the remoting revolution that's going on right now, taking it as a prompt to launch your own reinvention. Once we've convinced you of the merits and possibilities of reinventing yourself, we'll talk you through what you might want to consider as you embark on the remoting journey. Along the way, we'll provide you with a number of great resources that will support you as you start your personal reinvention, and onwards as you continue to thrive in your new remote life.

At the core of this book is the RETHiNK Remoting Model.

■ The RETHiNK Remoting Model

This is a 7-Part Model that we've developed over a number of years.

It's specifically designed for anyone who wants to work remotely as a means of enabling their personal reinvention, and it's never been more relevant than it is today.

The RETHiNK model is equally applicable whether you're already working remotely or have aspirations to eventually do so. It will be of interest whether you aspire to full-time or part-time remoting. It's designed to be helpful whether you are an employee with aspirations of developing a business on the side, or with the intention of eventually replacing your current job. It's even relevant if you already have your own business or businesses and want to adopt remoting into your working practices.

You will see, and likely also experience the world differently after you read this book and put its recommendations into action.

Let us introduce you to the 7 Part Model around which this book is structured, based on the acronym RETHiNK:

R - REINVENT

E - ENVIRONMENT

T - TOOLS

H - HEALTHZONE

I - INTEGRATE

N - NETWORK

K - KNOWLEDGE-BASE

This book is structured around a chapter that breaks down each element of the model.

Below we've provided a little taste of what each chapter covers.

R is for Reinvent

As mentioned already, remoting presents an opportunity to reinvent ourselves by redefining our approach to work and the ways in which we get things done, balanced around the rest of our lives.

Instead of spending precious hours every week crammed onto public transport or stuck in traffic, we can reinvest this time in ourselves and spend more precious time with our loved ones. We can take stock of what we value most and prioritise our efforts towards those things now so that we can avoid any regrets in the future.

Remoting can be the key that unlocks more of our time so that we can finally build our own business and become our own boss rather than working for a boss. This may involve building a side-venture, starting a business or beginning a process of education.

In whatever way you choose to reinvent yourself, remoting can be an enabler to make it happen.

E is for Environment

Our experience shows that in order to be successful in remoting, you must have the right setup that supports you in doing it - this starts with your working environment.

The right working environment correctly and comfortably equipped has a direct impact on your effectiveness, your efficiency, your energy and even how much you enjoy your work. Many who are reading this book will be starting out in their remoting adventure by working from home in their existing job. That in itself brings challenges, particularly if you're trying to repurpose an area within your home to make it into your workspace.

Apart from knowing what equipment you need to operate and thrive while remoting, you may also need to consider how to manage potential interruptions and disruptions caused by your partner, children or pets.

In this chapter we'll guide you through what you need in your working environment, and how to put it in place.

T is for Tools

An important element of our working environment is the tools that we use to get our work done with maximum efficiency and effectiveness. One factor that's often mentioned as a defence for working in an office is that the space is purposely designed for work, and fully equipped to maximise the productivity of its workers.

This isn't an insurmountable barrier to overcome, even if you're starting from scratch. Equipping ourselves for successful remoting doesn't mean having to spend vast sums of money on tools, technology or equipment. It doesn't require that we convert an area of our home, fitting it out with incongruous technology and office furniture.

In the tools chapter we'll look at some free and inexpensive equipment and software that will truly transform and maximise your productivity, enhance your onscreen presence for online meetings and presentations and equip you to produce high quality video should that be a part of your home business.

We'll also consider some of the technology requirements that working remotely brings into play – things that would be taken care of in a conventional office environment but which you may need to provide for yourself.

H is for Health Zone

You may have heard the expression that 'sitting is the new smoking'?

It derives from the notion that as human beings we've evolved over millions of years to live in bodies that are designed to move around. And yet, many knowledge workers in particular find themselves sitting for the majority of their working time in front of a screen and often not standing or moving for hours on end.

The effects of this are compounded by our largely sedentary lifestyle in leisure – many spend much of their free time sat on the couch watching TV or using their smartphones or tablets. They pacify themselves and appease their consciences with an occasional walk or workout.

Over time this level of inactivity has been shown by numerous studies to increase risk of diabetes, cardiovascular events including heart attacks and strokes, and early death - in effect, sitting can be almost as damaging to our health as smoking.

In this chapter then, our goal is to show you some simple and specific tactics and habits that you can use to stayed focused and energised so that you can avoid a negative impact on your health. We'll also talk about practices such as meditation, breathwork and routines to wind-down from work that are all helpful for reducing stress and switching off at the end of the working day.

I is for Integrate

As Aristotle put it "the whole is greater than the sum of its parts". In this chapter we will discuss how to bring all of the other elements of the model together, and illustrate why each of them is interlinked with and depends upon the others. When the parts of the RETHiNK model are working in unison, it yields the maximum benefit.

N is for Network

Working on your own can be lonely at times. The goal of remoting is to minimize wasted time and to eradicate distractions and interruptions so that you can reinvent yourself in whatever way you wish. But by no means is the intention that you become an isolated recluse in the process!

Some people thrive on being around their work colleagues and many socialise with co-workers, chatting over coffee or taking a lunchbreak together. Like it or not, many of us spend nearly as much time with those we work with, as those we choose to spend time with – our friends and family.

With remoting, such interpersonal contact can be lacking at times, or rather, much of it inevitably comes about through new channels – video conferencing and conference calls are two such models. Nonetheless, having a good network of people around you is really important, whether your interactions happen physically or virtually.

In this chapter we'll look at ways to avoid loneliness and to ensure that you continue to learn from and grow with others as you embark on your remoting journey. Having the support of others and being there to help others out too, are essential elements of successful remoting.

K is for Knowledge-base

The final part of the model is all about developing your knowledge-base and keeping up to date with developments and innovations that you can exploit and adopt in your remoting.

There are always new and exciting ways to work online with fresh opportunities to grow an online business, to learn, to make more money and to free up more of your time. In this chapter we'll reveal some ways to easily keep up to date as these opportunities emerge. We'll also signpost resources that you can obtain to remain appraised of new developments.

That's the RETHiNK Remoting model at a high level. Hopefully by now you're itching to get on and learn more? We're pleased to hear it.

Before we get started though, it's time for a couple of disclaimers and health warnings – bear with us.

As you'd hopefully expect, given that remoting is a relatively new concept that's heavily technology driven – quite a bit of what we discuss and advise within this book is based on what we know to be true, accurate and advisable right now.

It represents the accepted best practices and recommends the most useful and value-adding tools and technologies. Where appropriate, it also considers and complies with the legislation that prevails at the time of writing.

In the modern world however, things can change rapidly. What's true and recommended today, could become outdated tomorrow.

To counteract this, we encourage you to sign up and join our community so that you can keep up-to-date with developments and new opportunities as they emerge. Details on how to do this are provided in the chapter on Knowledge-base. If you want to get ahead of the game though, you can sign up here and now rather than waiting to do it later.

rethinkremoting.com

Finally, in relation to all content within the book regarding matters of health, it is important to point out that neither of us are qualified medical doctors. Our content is provided for informational purposes only, and you are advised to consult your own doctor before making any changes in your lifestyle and habits that could affect your health and wellbeing.

With all that said, let's move on.

In the next chapter we'll discuss the remote revolution and what it could mean for you; it's not just about doing the job you do today, remotely and removing the annoyances of the daily commute.

Instead, it's about completely redefining how you spend your time while working at your job or on your business. It's about leveraging the many additional opportunities and benefits offered by remoting for your own reinvention.

Intrigued? Read on and learn more!

The Remoting Revolution

Ⅰn the introduction we discussed some of the reasons why remoting has emerged as a viable and positive way of working, particularly for knowledge workers – those whose work involves handling and using information via online tools, applications and services. Before we dive into the details of the RETHiNK model and help you understand how to make remoting work for you, it seems worth taking a deeper dive into some of the key features of remoting. We will describe the effects that it can have in the lives of those who embrace it, and the considerations that need to be made when starting out with remoting.

To begin with, it may be worth considering what it is that actually makes our work meaningful. Understanding this makes it easy to see why remoting works so well for those who do it.

▪ The three characteristics of meaningful work

In the book 'Outliers' by Malcolm Gladwell, the author identified what he believes are the three essential ingredients that make our work feel meaningful. The same things apply whether we are working as an employee for someone else, whether we have our own business employing others, or whether we're an entrepreneur working on our own.

Those characteristics are as follows:

1) **Autonomy** – in our work we are free to choose how best to accomplish the task at hand (within reasonable parameters). We're not micromanaged and are left to our own devices to get the work done.

2) **Complexity** – our work is sufficiently engaging and challenging that we don't get bored or demoralised by having to do the same thing over and over again.

3) **A Connection between effort and reward** – there is a clear and obvious link between how hard we work, how diligently we apply ourselves and the rewards we receive for the effort that we put in.

With these three characteristics in mind, have a think about some of the jobs you've done in the past. Feel free to go back in your life as far as you'd like, too.

Think back to your first job. Perhaps you worked in a shop or supermarket as a teenager. For many of us, such jobs didn't incorporate much of any of the three elements above.

We were told what to do and how to do it. The work was tedious and repetitive. It made little difference how hard we worked – we'd still get paid the same amount per hour regardless. The only link between effort and reward might have been that if we didn't work hard enough, we'd be fired! Perhaps then, there was a link between effort and reward after all!

Next, think about a job you've had or a business you've run more recently. Consider again whether it ticked the boxes for all three characteristics above. If you enjoyed autonomy, the work was interesting and the rewards you earned could be affected by working harder (a simple example would be the possibility of a bonus as a reward for going above and beyond the call of duty), then it's likely the work felt meaningful and significant.

Do you now see how important these elements are? We can tolerate jobs that aren't meaningful if, for example, we make a lot of money at them but they will still lack meaning at a fundamental level. If all three elements aren't present then chances are it'll be hard to commit to the work over a longer period of time and it won't feel as meaningful as we'd like.

Now let's look at remoting through the lens of whether or not it makes our work meaningful.

Autonomy – If we're working remotely, whether at home or in a shared workspace, chances are we're not going to have our boss, employees or business partners looking over our shoulders. We'll be given our work to do and will largely be left to our own devices to prioritise tasks and to choose how we do them. *Remoting enables autonomy in our work.*

Complexity – Remoting doesn't necessarily mean that our work becomes more technically taxing or stimulating, but the beauty of remoting is that we have more freedom to pursue other things to enrich our day and to get more out of our time. Without direct supervision we might look for new and innovative ways to get our work done more quickly and efficiently so that we have more free time. We might choose to build a business alongside our job, making use of slack time. We might undertake some private study or personal development work in between tasks. *Remoting can be the means of adding complexity and stimulation into our daily lives – something that might be difficult to do in a conventional working environment.*

Connection between effort and reward – This is where remoting can really come into its own. The opportunity to pursue other ventures and personal growth is facilitated by remoting. When we take advantage of remoting to either free up time by working in a way that suits us better, or pursue opportunities to earn more money alongside our work, or to learn and grow, there's a clear link between the rewards we receive and the efforts we put in. *Remoting allows us to earn greater reward from the efforts put in during our working lives.*

Hopefully you can now see that even if we were merely to adopt remoting as a means of doing a job that is currently done in an office, there are opportunities to make that work more meaningful just by moving to a remote setting.

We'll likely enjoy greater autonomy, freedom to broaden our horizons and have the chance to earn greater reward for our efforts – either more free time, or more money from other ventures – or maybe even both!

Now let's dive into some of the many other beneficial effects that can result from remoting.

◼ Time savings

Earlier, we discussed the time savings that can be unlocked with remoting, but these cannot be over-stated and we'll likely refer to these on many occasions throughout this book. Time is our most precious and scarce resource – we cannot make more of it and when it's gone, it cannot be captured and re-used.

For this reason, our time is worth protecting and shouldn't be wasted where we can help it.

For individuals and businesses alike, time can be saved by remoting. Here are just a few examples of how:

- Reduced commuting (which also saves money and reduces environmental pollution by eradicating unnecessary journeys).

- Medical appointments, parent/teacher meetings and other personal errands that would otherwise require time out from the working day can be fit-in more easily and with less disruption.

- Less useful working time is lost through needlessly being dragged into meetings that are irrelevant, or through interruptions and distractions caused by other people.

These are just three common examples – you'll likely have others that are more pertinent to your working life.

The time saved is an obvious factor that makes remoting a compelling prospect. For many, saving time on the commute alone is enough of a reason to consider it seriously.

■ It promotes mental and physical health

Since the pandemic, many employers are far more conscious of helping their employees to protect their mental and physical health. When normal life was disrupted so suddenly and to such a severe extent, employers recognised that their staff needed to be supported and given flexibility and freedom rather than being burdened with stress and heightened expectations.

During the pandemic, many employers recognised that their workers appreciated being given flexibility and freedom of choice to set their own working patterns (within reason). It was clear that empowering and trusting people to get the job done without micro-managing them brought out the best in many. It gave people freedom to do things that they found helpful to their mental and physical health, and to slot whatever habits and practices were necessary around their work, as a means of keeping body and mind in good health.

Some found it beneficial to take regular walks. Some exercised, meditated or incorporated yoga into their daily routines. Others just made sure to take regular time away from their work at regular intervals throughout the day. Many employers found it a good reason to block out their employees' calendars for an hour each lunchtime to encourage remote workers to actually take a lunchbreak.

It seems remarkable that many of these ideas seem innovative or revolutionary. It shouldn't be a big deal to encourage workers to take time away from the computer to get some fresh air or eat lunch, and yet many had become used to going without such things. It took a global pandemic for many to realise the importance of doing the basics well.

Remoting proved to be the ideal catalyst for helping us recognise this.

While many of these things could have been promoted or facilitated in an office environment, they are universally suited to those working remotely and are often easier to fit in when working from home.

Take something like exercise – if you intended to exercise during your lunchbreak as an office worker, you'd need to pack your sports gear the night before and take it with you on your commute. You'd need to have exercise facilities close to your office so that you had time to get there, do your workout and get back afterwards. You'd need somewhere to change before and afterwards. And if you were just going for a run from the office, you'd still need changing facilities that your employer might not provide. You'd probably want to take a shower afterwards too.

And you'd usually be constrained to getting it all done inside an hour that's typically allotted to lunch by most employers.

For someone who's remoting, few of these constraints exist. Exercise can be fit in around work and getting changed before and after can too. There's little need for preparation, other than to make sure your gear is to hand, and your calendar blocked out for your exercise time. Exercise is fit in seamlessly around other tasks, and there's no guilt or stress in doing so.

The same goes for activities like meditation. It may be possible to find a quiet room in an office building within which to spend a few minutes meditating and doing breath-work. It's unlikely to be as relaxing an experience as sitting in a quiet space at home, where there's no risk of being disturbed. At home we can easily close the door and take the time out of our working day, free from distractions to meditate without interruption. Our mind is calmed as a result, and we're better equipped for the rigours of the day.

Having the flexibility to do things that prioritise mental and physical health around our work, is another significant benefit of remoting.

■ Remoting helps avoid unnecessary meetings

An insidious aspect of office life is the number and length of meetings that are set-up, demanding the time of multiple attendees who often have little to offer or gain from them.

Such meetings often prevent attendees from doing anything else, and yet few who are invited feel emboldened to decline an invite for fear of missing out, or because they don't want to appear unimportant or detached.

Many who set up such meetings or attend them, do so as a means of building and projecting their status – not because they genuinely feel the meeting will make a valuable contribution to the business. In-person meetings also tend to run for as long as they are scheduled rather than finishing early if there's nothing further to discuss. Without a clear agenda and an effective chairperson, in-person meetings can overrun and achieve nothing other than wasting the time of those attending and money for the business in lost productivity.

Remote meetings on the other hand - whether held over audio or video – tend to be shorter and more focussed. They don't usually run for longer than necessary since it's a lot harder for people to take the discussion off track when only one person can speak and be heard at a time.

There's less danger of such meetings being hijacked by one person with an agenda of their own. Remote meetings also allow information to be shared and disseminated to large groups efficiently using presentations and screen sharing. Remote meetings negate the need to gather everyone together in one place. Recordings can be taken and distributed to those who couldn't make the session.

Finally, while multi-tasking is falling out of vogue and is often equated with doing multiple things badly – it is possible to join a remote meeting and get on with other tasks while waiting for a particular agenda item that requires your input. This seems like a better use of your time rather than attending for the duration and having to wait patiently until you're needed.

■ Remoting allows for fewer disruptions and interruptions

In an office environment people are much more likely to stop by at your desk-side and hover, hoping they can ask you a quick question. Some people seem to wander around open plan offices in search of gossip or social chat instead of getting on with their work.

They overlook that the people they stop and interrupt to speak with, could have been engrossed in deep work and don't want to chat, but also don't want to appear rude.

Many who defend working in an office will claim that spontaneous conversations can lead to great ideas, which may be true to an extent. But when you're remoting you have the choice to start such conversations when it's convenient, and to concentrate on a task when you need to give it your undivided attention.

Remote working tools and technologies such as instant messaging allow people to reach out spontaneously and in real-time, but as the recipient you still have the choice over whether and when to respond. Such tools also usually allow a status to be set (e.g. 'Do Not Disturb') which helps to minimise disruptions – this can be a real benefit when concentrating deeply on a task.

▪ It enables financial savings

Remoting can be a way of saving significant sums of money, not just for the individual but also for businesses that would otherwise have to provide office facilities, computer equipment, furniture and staffing (including security, cleaners and so-on).

For individuals, the sources of potential savings are numerous:

- **Commuting costs** - train and bus tickets, car parking, fuel and so-on

- **Food and drinks** – whether you favour a green smoothie or a few cappuccinos each day, you can make these at home rather than buying them at a café. Healthy and nutritious lunches can be prepared at home, rather than buying a sandwich at the shop or cafeteria.

- **Reduced need for work clothes** – if you had to wear business dress to the office, you'll need less of it if you're remoting most of the time. A couple of smart outfits may suffice for wearing on video calls and even then, only on the top half of you that's visible on screen! Even if your business involves recording videos, you'll still need less 'business clothing'. You may save on dry cleaning and laundry costs too.

- **Lowered childcare costs** – Your commute may have prevented you from getting home in time to collect your children from school, but remoting potentially removes this issue. You may feel happier knowing that you're home when your children get back from school. Depending on the age and independence of your kids, you might not need to employ a childminder or nanny any longer.

The savings vary from one person to the next, but these are just a few examples that will apply to many.

■ It helps avoid *wasting* time

We've already talked about the ways that remoting can save time. But there's also time that gets wasted in the course of a typical working day.

Few would credibly argue that sitting in a traffic jam is a good use of time. Even if you use the time to listen to audiobooks or educational podcasts, that time could be better spent before or after work, taking a daily walk and consuming the same content while exercising. Alternatively, the time could be used taking care of chores at home and keeping life on track.

Remoting is a means of taking time that was previously wasted or which detracted from your day and repurposing it for positive gains.

While cynics may fear that remote employees will do less work, it has been proven that with fewer distractions and a greater incentive to get work done, that productivity and output of many workers actually increases.

Tasks no-longer extend unnecessarily to use up the time available (in line with Parkinson's Law). The incentive exists to get our work done as efficiently as possible, particularly if remoting is intended to assist in our reinvention. By getting our work done more efficiently we are then free to get on with other tasks that contribute to that reinvention, to build our business or better ourselves through education and personal development.

Remoting also provides the flexibility to work to our own schedule (within reason).

Many knowledge workers have learned that they don't need to be constrained to a conventional, 9-to-5 window for work, and yet office environments tend to operate around such a schedule.

Through remoting, it's possible for early risers to log on and start their work as soon as they're awake and ready for the day, potentially finishing earlier too if that's in-line with their other goals and commitments.

Those who prefer a more leisurely start to the day are able to start late and work later into the day.

Fundamentally, remoting enables greater freedom of choice over how we live our lives and get our work done. It helps us to avoid wasting time.

■ It puts work-life balance to the fore

Long-term remote workers often describe how they've structured their working day around other aspects of their lives – incorporating and prioritizing their highest values.

- It may be a priority for them to drop their children at school in the morning and pick them up at night.

- It may be important for them to be home for dinner with the family each evening.

- They may want to exercise at lunchtime each day, since that's when they have the most energy.

- Their preference may be to break the working day into chunks, taking more than half an hour or an hour in the middle of the day.

Achieving work-life balance is also about making sure that the things that we need to get done are balanced with being able to do the things we want to do.

There's a clichéd perspective on remoting that presumes that home workers use time when they should be working to do housework and chores instead. The notion is that when the working day ends, they're free to relax as they've got their chores done while working.

Is this really such a ridiculous idea?

By virtue of being at home, it's often possible to get chores done in parallel to working. Both get done during the course of the day, without impacting upon our ability to be productive and successful in our job or as we build our business.

Some examples of doing this in practice might include;

- Running the washing machine and hanging clothes out to dry in between tasks, or while taking a break from work

- Arranging for groceries to be delivered during the working day so that we can put them away during a break

- Opting for cheaper, flexible delivery slots for online orders, safe in the knowledge we'll be home to receive them

- Being home to allow tradespeople, cleaners, gardeners or any other help that we might enlist, to do their work without having to make convoluted arrangements for their access

We all have chores and personal-admin tasks that are necessary to keep our lives on-track and our households running smoothly. Remoting can help us to gradually get these things done in parallel to or around our work throughout the day. Once we finish work, our families are home and our time is our own. We can truly focus on relaxing with them rather than being distracted by the chores that still need doing.

The nature of each person's work will determine how flexible they can be when organising their day. But generally speaking, remoting makes it easier to achieve a balance between the demands presented by our work and those that emerge from our lives more generally.

■ Summing up

In this chapter we've discussed a few of the many beneficial effects that can be expected from remoting. If you were in any doubt over whether it was worth pursuing, hopefully by now you're convinced.

If your employer, business partner or even your family were uncertain about how it might work and why you might be interested in remoting, then hopefully some of these benefits can help you to convince them too.

Perhaps the most exciting side-effect of remoting is in the opportunity it enables for reinventing ourselves. This reinvention could come about in many ways and in different areas of our lives. In the next chapter, we'll talk you through how this could emerge.

It's time to start exploring the RETHiNK Remoting model, beginning with Reinvention. Are you ready to take back the remote control of your life?

Reinvent

The letter R in the RETHiNK Remoting model stands for Reinvent.

As mentioned in the opening chapters, people all over the world are realising that the remote revolution has begun, presenting us all with an unmissable opportunity to reinvent ourselves.

It is allowing us to reinvent how we live, how we work, where we work from and indeed *who* we work for.

Many people have had a remote revelation and realised that if they can work online at home for someone else, perhaps they could work for themselves instead (or as well).

After all, the dictionary defines reinvent as *'to change something so much that it appears to be entirely new'*, an example being *'to take up a radically new job or way of life'*.

Imagine for a moment working in a job that doesn't involve running to jump on to a packed train or wasting precious time stuck in traffic at the start and end of each day. A world where you can have breakfast with loved ones every morning and start your work minutes later. A life where you are able to fit in exercise around your work with ease, able to prepare and enjoy healthy food during the working day instead of having to grab a sandwich from the cafeteria. An existence where work and life are in perfect balance and you aren't constantly stressed about meeting the demands of your work, home and family lives.

Remoting is the key to such a life. It's a means of unlocking precious time and of enabling choices that help us to prioritise our highest values.

We can use the time and new-found freedom that remoting unlocks to reinvent ourselves; to rethink how we might improve our health, our wealth, our relationships and our community.

For those considering starting a side-project or their own business, remoting is particularly relevant. Remoting can be the perfect catalyst for starting such projects.

■ Understanding your values

The first step that we invite you to take in the process of reinventing yourself, is to get clear on your values. If you've done this already, you'll know how powerful the exercise is.

Even if you've done it before, there's no harm in going through it once again.

It's widely-accepted that to enjoy a great life that's lived with integrity and feels fulfilling, our actions must align with our values. When we're living in line with our innate core values, this is when we can be said to be being completely true to ourselves.

The great Dr John Demartini states that our values arise from our conscious or unconscious voids – that is, the thing (or things) which we perceive as most lacking in our life.

The void that's left by the things that we feel are missing from our life becomes the thing that we perceive as most important. In this way, it is signalled as our highest value.

■ What is your highest value?

Let's take 60-seconds to reflect. Close your eyes and think about what you feel is missing from your life and what, by definition, is most important to you?

Did you find it hard to choose just one thing? If you thought of a few, then make a list and assign each item a number starting with 1 (most important), then number 2 (next-most important) and so-on. That exercise could help bring into focus the thing or things that correspond to your highest values.

Here's another quick exercise to help you understand your highest values and what matters most to you.

Grab a pen and some paper and put in some time and thought to complete the 4 simple statements that follow.

Admiration

I admire	Name
Because they	

Inspiration

I get really inspired when I	Describe what it is you are doing
Because I feel	Describe what is happening

Stimulation

I feel most alive when I	Describe what it is you are doing
Because I feel	

Association

I feel most like myself when I am with	Name
Because they make me feel	

Once you have done this exercise, ask yourself - does your life align with the values that you've identified as being most important to you? Do your answers to these questions suggest that your life feels fulfilled and accomplished and is spent doing the things that inspire you with people you admire? Or are you spending the majority of your time suffering through things and feeling little in the way of joy and fulfilment?

If your life doesn't align with the values that the exercise has revealed as being most important to you, then this is the perfect place to start reinventing yourself.

You can start by using what used to be your commuting time, to undertake new activities that align more closely with your values. We are going to presume that sleeping-in is not your highest value. Devoting the time that you've saved from commuting to doing something that is stimulating, fulfilling, exciting and feels worthwhile will give you a greater sense of joy, since it'll be a step closer to meeting your values. Such examples could include:

- Spending that extra time writing, painting or sketching before work, to exercise your creativity

- Using the time to generate ideas for the business that you'd like to start, and to then start the work of creating it

- Using the time to exercise so that you enjoy the feeling of using your body and burning energy

- Taking a regular morning walk with a friend, or your spouse to begin each day with someone who enriches your life

Using the time saved from commuting provides an immediate payback from remoting that will likely enhance the quality of your life from the get-go.

The next part of reinventing yourself that has a massive impact on everything else is to consider your work.

Ask yourself a few simple questions about what you do for work today:

- Does your job align with your values?

- Does it give you the freedom that you crave - both financial freedom and the time to fill the voids and address your values?

If the answer is no, then as we already mentioned the remoting revolution may be the means by which you unlock the time to start a new online business of your own.

Let's take a look at the ways that reinvention could manifest in your life. The process of reinvention is about using remoting as an enabler to make whatever changes are necessary in your life to align what you do and who you are, with your highest values.

Learning and education

In years gone by, education and training tended to happen in the early part of our lives. We progressed through education – from school, to college and perhaps university.

At each step we specialised more and more until fully qualified to work in our chosen field. For other professions we might have gone from full-time education into an apprenticeship or training scheme where some of the learning was done on the job.

Many people invested years of their lives, and often thousands of dollars in the process of becoming fully educated and trained. The debt they carried into their career often lasted for a lot longer than their enjoyment of the work did.

Contemplating a radical change of career or a personal reinvention was too daunting to ever consider. It may mean going back to the beginning, returning to study, and dropping several rungs down the career (and earning) ladder. It would probably represent the loss of a few years of learning and experience, writing off the benefit of work they'd put in to build their previous career.

For many, this was too much of a backwards step to contemplate and so they remained stuck in jobs they really didn't like or which they'd grown disinterested in.

Now more than ever before, there are opportunities all around us to learn new subjects and master new skills. Whether our return to learning is prompted out of curiosity or intended to achieve a level of mastery so that we can monetise our new knowledge, there has never been so much information so readily available as there is today.

It's not only the volume of information that's changed in recent years – there are new ways to learn and new channels through which to access information as well. Webinars, membership sites, email lists and online training courses all allow us to benefit from the wisdom and skills possessed by others. This shift means changing how we approach learning altogether:

- If you want to learn something now, do you begin by looking at what courses are offered at your local college or university, or do you go to Google and search for courses and webinars that are available online?

- If you want to learn how to do something technical, do you reach for the phonebook and call a qualified professional to train you, or do you visit YouTube to see if someone has recorded and uploaded an instructional video?

- If you want to understand a new subject do you buy a few books and try to digest the contents, or do you seek out blog posts and articles that have been published online by credible sources and experts, sampling what's available for free?

We may descend deep into the rabbit hole, seeking out ever-more detailed information on a topic. This might lead us to formal study and accreditation through sitting exams. At other times, we'll use 'just in time learning' to equip us with the skills or knowledge for the task at hand. It's so easy now to find out what we want to know within minutes, and often we can get at least a taster of the deeper learning for free or with minimal expenditure.

As content creators we also have the opportunity to monetise our knowledge and skills by creating and selling video training courses to others. We'll cover this in more detail, later in the book. If this is your particular area of interest then you may want to get a head start and pick up a copy of the book *Say It Once. Sell It Often.'* which deals specifically with that very topic.

Remoting can be an enabler to pursuing education and learning, potentially alongside our existing work by making best use of the free time that inevitably crops-up between tasks. In a conventional job or office environment, training would typically be confined to time allocated to sanctioned online training courses, or perhaps attendance at an in-person training for a few days each year.

What we mean by this is that if you work for a bank (for example), they're not likely to approve you studying a foreign language alongside your work unless it's going to benefit their business. If you're remoting, you're more likely to be able to carve out the time in your schedule to study that language for your own interest and growth, alongside your work.

When you're reinventing yourself through remoting, there are fewer barriers to prevent you from indulging your curiosity and passion for learning. This is the time to investigate and explore, pursuing your passions and indulging your interests.

This will help to expand your mind and your skillset. It may well lead you to your next business venture too.

◾ It enables side-projects and entrepreneurial ventures

If you've ever tried to start a business or build up a side-hustle, you'll likely be aware of the debate over whether to quit your existing job so you're completely free to focus on your new venture, or to do both in parallel. Most of us have bills to pay, and it can often feel more comfortable to hang onto the job so we can cover our expenses.

The flip-side of this safety-net is that by keeping our job, the time available for our new project is limited.

We all have the same number of hours in the day to use as we see fit, but it can take real discipline to use our free time for educating ourselves or improving our situation by starting a business when we're having to do it outside of working hours.

You may want to escape your job but don't want to lose the safety net of income that your job provides until your business is more mature and making sufficient money to support you. It can be hard to keep a job going while devoting attention to building your business as well, particularly when you're going into an office environment on a daily basis and can't be seen to be doing anything that might be seen as detracting from your job (even if it isn't).

Remoting while you do your job (presumably to the best of your ability, as the conscientious and diligent person you are) is a good way of making better use of the lulls in demand and the occasional down time that inevitably comes up between tasks in everyone's work. It's by using these moments of 'free time' as they occur during the working day, that we can start devoting time to our reinvention.

■ The death of 'busy-work'

In an office environment, workers often feel a pressure to appear busy so as to justify their position and to appear important amongst colleagues. They might busy themselves with low-importance tasks or take longer than necessary to do jobs that could have been done quickly.

They might spin out projects by calling unnecessary meetings so-as to appear important. The net effect is that there's plenty of time that's not used productively other than by keeping busy, and it serves little useful purpose as a result.

With remoting there's no incentive to appear busy since there's nobody there to impress or convince of your theoretical importance.

A good employer will be more concerned with ensuring that their employees are doing the job they're paid to do to the best of their ability, not just whether they're putting in the requisite 7 or 8 hours per day or appearing busy during that time. Knowledge workers are usually employed to deliver projects or to get things done – not to put in a set number of hours each day.

Remoting allows us to focus on doing tasks to the best of our ability and as efficiently as possible. Busy-work ceases to be a factor and often this shift in ethos means that plenty of time is freed up in the course of the working day. This time can be put towards training or education, to work on side-projects or put towards some other worthy endeavour.

■ What sorts of business opportunity exist?

The kinds of business model that are best suited to this kind of venture are constantly evolving. It may vary based on online trends and evolving technologies.

You can make sure that you remain in-touch with the kinds of business model that are suitable for those who want to reinvent themselves as business owners, by joining our network, via the link below:

rethinkremoting.com

The sorts of venture that you might consider building into businesses alongside your work, and which can be easily fit-in around other jobs and progressed with just a few hours of effort each week, include the following examples:

Social Media Marketing – The key principle of this business model is to build up a profile, a following and an email list corresponding to those followers by leveraging the reach enabled by social media platforms. The following grows as you demonstrate skills, knowledge or expertise in a particular niche or business area. Once you have a following on Facebook, Twitter or other similar platforms, you can monetise that audience by recommending affiliate products and services that are relevant to the niche, via social media and emails to your list. This business model can only generate money if you also deliver value in the form of free content to the audience too. Bear in mind that this, like all businesses, demands investment of time and effort and won't happen overnight. To learn more, please follow the link below.

rethinkremoting.com

Recording and selling online video training courses/Creating a membership site – This is about using modern technology to package and sell digital training products – video, audio and text - that can be sold over and over again as a means of packaging your knowledge and skills, to benefit others. Whether you sell your content on a platform such as Udemy, Thinkific, Teachable or Gumroad, or choose instead to host your own site where your courses are sold, the aim of this business is to create a product that can be sold multiple times, and which remains evergreen. To learn more about creating online training courses, please follow the link below.

rethinkremoting.com

Selling white-label goods via Amazon or Shopify – For many years now it has been possible to source white-label products from manufacturers overseas, and for these to then be sold via Amazon and fulfilled from Amazon warehouses. A similar business model is to use drop-shipping to sell goods on the Shopify platform. The set-up of such businesses can often involve a fair amount of initial training and investment up front, but the financial rewards can be significant once the processes are automated and the passive income is flowing.

Start a Podcast – Using a free podcasting platform such as Anchor. fm you can record and broadcast your own podcast on a topic of your choice. With little technical effort it's possible to reach and build a global audience of listeners. This can then be monetised by seeking sponsorships, running adverts and promoting products to subscribers. As with many of these business models, there are overlaps with the others – a podcast can be a useful element of a social media marketing business for example.

Providing Services via the Gig Economy – Using platforms such as UpWork and Fiverr it's possible to sell your skills and time to a global audience, taking on freelance work that's completed while working remotely. Services that are in high-demand include graphic design, web design, video editing, ghost writing and text editing, and creation and formatting of online digital content. The sites above (and others like them) allow freelancers to bid for work advertised by prospective clients, and also allow creators to advertise their services in a centralised marketplace.

Blogging and Vlogging – Using a blog or vlog you can position yourself as a subject matter expert on a topic of your choice by writing or videoing valuable original content and curating other content that complements your own. Monetisation is achieved by building a base of followers and subscribers, and by servicing an email list. You can also include affiliate links with your content and within emails to your list as a means of generating income. Advertising and sponsorship can come as a result of building a large following.

Live online teaching and tutoring – Ever since the global pandemic we've become more used to meeting and interacting with others using online meeting platforms such as Zoom and Microsoft Teams. These technologies have made it easier than ever to deliver live video lessons and training to others. You may wish to offer tutoring to school kids, or perhaps you have a skillset that's suitable for offering to individuals or groups of adults. Either way, this can quickly be turned into a profitable business with almost no outlay of money. It's another way of monetising your skills, knowledge and expertise.

▪ Summing up

These are just a few of the business models you could choose to adopt and the opportunities that can open up for those who want to make the best use of their time while remoting. If you crave the freedom and autonomy of being your own boss, think about starting your own business using one of these online models. The key is to choose one and get started as soon as possible.

The types of business could vary over time as new trends and technologies emerge. For further details on these and other businesses, please follow the link below.

rethinkremoting.com

For now, suffice to say that remoting is a means of ensuring that we have the greatest opportunity to make the best use of every moment of every day, whatever we might be working at in our lives. The key is to get started on your own Reinvention, TODAY.

Environment

The letter E in the RETHiNK Remoting Model stands for Environment.

Being set up for successful remoting begins with establishing the ideal working environment. The space in which you work has the potential to influence your effectiveness, your efficiency, your energy and even how much you enjoy your work.

What we are going to cover in this chapter applies whether you're working remotely online for someone else or for yourself. In short, it's about your workspace itself, not what you do within it!

■ Establishing your workspace

For the purposes of this chapter, we'll be assuming that you are setting yourself up for remoting within your home. A little later we'll discuss the concept of co-working spaces too, but right now this is about preparing a space in your home where you can work.

It starts with identifying and creating a designated working space - ideally in a spare room or somewhere 'off the beaten track' in your home - that gets you in the right frame of mind for work and allows you to concentrate when you're in a flow state.

In other words, it'll ideally be a space that you don't use for anything else. We know the kitchen table is a popular option for many who come to remoting, but if you can avoid this then please do. Having a designated space trains your brain to recognise that you're in your place of work where you will be productive and won't be so easily distracted. It's the same principle as preparing ourselves to exercise by putting on our sports gear or picking up our dog's lead to signal to them that it's time for a walk. The more cues we can give ourselves or others, the better the outcomes we'll get – that holds for how we equip ourselves for successful remoting.

What's even better about having a devoted space for remoting is that if you can physically close the home-office door behind you and switch off the lights when you finish for the day, it really helps to delineate and differentiate between your work and personal life.

If you don't have the space at home, or this is simply not physically possible, that's okay too. If your desk is located in the corner of your bedroom and that is where you will do your work, then try to compartmentalise that space mentally anyway. When you're sat at the desk, you're at work, but once you step away from it for the day, you're home.

Building this separation in your mind demands telling yourself regularly "When I am not at my desk, I am not working". It may take some time to engrain that belief, but it's time well spent.

■ Managing others' expectations

You've likely seen the viral videos on social media where people have been deeply engrossed in a video call or an interview, and a child or unwitting partner has suddenly barged into the room, disturbing the peace. While such videos are amusing, they highlight a problem that can arise if there isn't sufficient space in the home for your workspace or if others in the household are allowed to wander in unannounced.

Remoting was particularly difficult during the pandemic, when children were home schooling, and nobody could leave the home. Everyone had to make compromises and make the lack of space work as best they could.

But now that things are returning back to normal, your workspace should be defined, delineated and ideally respected by others in the household, as somewhere you go to do work. A 'Do Not Disturb' or 'Genius at Work' sign on the door can work wonders.

If there are other people in the house, try to use the quietest room available as your workspace. Ideally you should avoid working in a room adjacent to the bathroom or laundry room, for example.

Furniture for your workspace

We recommend that you have a working area of at least 2 square meters, ideally in a room that is bigger than that.

Within this working area should be your desk, ideally 1 square meter (or greater) and a comfortable chair designed for sitting at a desk. We've already discussed the notion that sitting is the new smoking, and for this reason we strongly suggest that you stand for regular periods throughout the working day. A sit-stand desk is well worth the investment If this is an option for you.

When sitting it is important to adopt and comply with principles of ergonomics.

1. You should sit with your back straight with your shoulders relaxed

2. Your thighs should be fully supported by the chair

3. The top of your computer screen should be at, or slightly below eye level

4. Your lower back should be supported by the chair

5. Your forearms should be at 90 degrees to your back

6. Your feet should be flat on the floor or you should use a footrest

7. Your screen should be at least an arm's length away from you

Ideally, the room you work in should have a window to allow natural light and fresh air in. It's important that you are able to control the amount of light getting in with a blind or curtains, particularly when you're on a video call or recording videos. Don't set up your desk so that you're constantly going to be fighting glare, reflections or shadows because of a poorly-situated desk.

With this in mind we recommend that you have a number of LED lights available to luminate your workspace so that you can adjust the brightness depending on what you're doing, and regardless of whether it's light or dark outside.

We will cover this in more detail in the chapter on Tools.

As most remote working can involve regular online meetings it's really important to reduce echo within the space. This is especially important if you deliver online training and webinars or record videos for marketing or as part of online courses.

Echo can be reduced by putting down a rug, adding more furniture to the room or hanging heavier curtains over the windows. You can also use acoustic foam panels on the walls and ceiling or use free-standing ones instead if you don't want to fully and permanently convert your home.

■ Helping yourself to avoid distractions

One of the more common reservations that many express about remoting is whether they would find it possible to concentrate with so many potential distractions around them. There are of course distractions all around us in our homes. Avoiding distraction merely requires that we choose not to allow ourselves to be lured by them:

- The refrigerator full of food

- The laundry that needs to be done

- The TV and the couch luring us to sit and relax

- The child wanting us to play with them

- The spouse who wants us to give them our attention

You get the picture.

There's no substitute for a bit of discipline and resolve. But we can set ourselves up for success by establishing a few basic ground-rules that we'll commit to following as part of our remoting experience.

- While food may be readily available, it's wise to stick with the same eating patterns as you'd normally follow while working (more on this in the Healthzone chapter). Stick a post-it note saying 'WHAT NOW?' on the fridge door if it helps to discourage you from opening it regularly in search of snacks!

- If you work best with a bit of music in the background, then this can be a real opportunity enabled by remoting. Put on whatever music you like at whatever volume suits you, as long as it's conducive to doing your best work. There are limits though - few people seem to do their best work with the TV on in the background for example. If that's the case for you, commit to leaving the TV switched off if there's one in your home office – or preferably don't have one in there at all if you're prone to distraction.

In the episode on Tools, we'll look at other ways to stay focused and avoid distraction with some apps that will really help. The key message though, is that if you're likely to be distracted by something (even as innocuous as a picture on the wall) – then remove it from your workspace.

■ Lighting

Designers of office spaces will spend an enormous amount of time (and money) ensuring that offices are well-lit, to the correct intensity and from the right places and most appropriate sources. It's important that workers don't suffer from glare on their screens or eyestrain from excessively dull or bright conditions.

Homes don't tend to be designed or lit with the same considerations in mind however. Bedrooms may be naturally darker than an office space. Conversely, modern living spaces are often designed to maximise natural light.

When preparing your space for remoting, it may be worth experimenting with the placement of your desk and with some different light sources. Place these in different locations relative to your desk and screen such that you can enjoy optimum lighting.

We'll discuss lighting for video calls and recording of video content separately, but the aim generally is to light your workspace adequately without making it feel like a film set!

As always, for health and environmental reasons too, it makes sense to maximise the natural light within your workspace. If natural light is limited where you're remoting, it's always worth taking regular breaks to absorb sunlight as often as your work allows. A few minutes of getting the sun on our skin can have enormously beneficial impacts on our health and our mood.

■ Temperature control

Large office spaces don't tend to offer much flexibility for workers wanting to control the temperature. Conversely, in smaller shared spaces it can be easy for 'thermostat wars' to break out between those who like the office warm with the heating on permanently, and those who prefer a cooler environment with fresh air circulating.

The beauty of remoting is that you get to choose how warm or cool your workspace is – if you want the window wide open in mid-December, go for it!

Beware though, there can be a tendency if you're home-alone to resist or avoid heating or cooling the whole house. It feels like a waste of money and an environmentally-damaging choice to put the heating or air-conditioning on when you're the only person home, and yet it can hinder productivity and comfort to suffer excessive heat or cold.

We suggest investing in a good quality, energy-efficient space heater or fan for use in your home office. It doesn't have to be on at all times, but your comfort will play a direct role on your productivity and you deserve not to suffer in the name of economy! The environmental impacts of an energy-efficient heater or fan will also be limited.

■ Background noise

A final environmental consideration around remoting is in whether you prefer to work in silence, or with background noise. We touched upon this earlier when discussing distractions, but it warrants a little extra thought.

In an office, background hubbub is unavoidable, whether that's the photocopier whirring, phones ringing or social conversations echoing between desks.

Some find it easier to deal with background noise by working with earphones in, whether to cancel out the background or for listening to certain kinds of music that they find promotes focus.

It's a matter of individual choice of course, but when you're remoting you have the freedom to set the environmental background noise to suit you. You may like having the radio on for company and entertainment. You might favour having your favourite band or composer's music playing over your stereo. Others still may prefer wearing noise-cancelling headphones even if they're home alone, with ambient music or binaural beats (a particular kind of music that's been proven to encourage concentration and productivity) playing while they focus on the task at hand.

Remoting provides an opportunity to experiment without fear of offending or inconveniencing anyone else! You may discover that a particular artist or genre of music brings out your creative and productive side!

■ Co-working space

An alternative to working from home is to use a co-working space. This offers much of the flexibility of remoting at home, but also provides the structure of a designated place of business that some need to be able to work, even if they're not going to their own company's office.

Co-working spaces provide a great opportunity to vary your working environment and also to meet and network with new people, potentially from other diverse businesses and industries. They're also useful if you need to arrange occasional face-to-face meetings with project teams or for sales purposes – a bit more professional than inviting a prospect round to meet in your spare bedroom!

Co-working spaces can be especially helpful when the line between work and home starts to blur – a danger that we mentioned earlier.

There are many businesses around the world that are dedicated to created co-working spaces and these are becoming more commonplace in towns and city centres, particularly post-pandemic. Many organisations have realised that they don't need a dedicated office for their staff and that it makes sense to co-locate with other businesses and entrepreneurs who all share the same basic requirements; a clean and secure, furnished office space, with a decent internet connection.

A co-working space provides all these facilities and services, with the added bonus of there being other knowledge workers who are also remoting there and who can provide the social contact that we all crave from time-to-time. We'll discuss the importance of this further in the chapter covering Network.

■ Summing up

The key takeaway here is that you'll find that remoting to be far more effective and beneficial if you've established a comfortably furnished, designated workspace. Giving due consideration to your remoting environment helps you to enjoy working as well as feeling comfortable, productive and focussed.

In the next chapter we'll explore some of the essential Tools that will compliment your working environment.

Tools

The letter T in the RETHiNK Remoting Model stands for Tools. In the previous chapter we spoke about the importance of the establishing the right working environment that supports you in remoting effectively. The tools we use within this environment play an important role in successful remoting too. In this chapter we'll be introducing the foundational tools that will help you thrive in your remoting revolution.

The key tools fall into a number of categories:

- Internet Access

- Computer (software and security)

- Project Management and Time Management

- Simple Studio Setup

■ Internet Access

At the height of the pandemic, many families came to realise how much we rely on our internet connection throughout our work, education and leisure. When your work relies upon being able to access online services as well as using the internet for voice and video communications, it can quickly expose the frailties and inadequacies of weaker internet connections.

Top of the list then when putting the tools in place for remoting is a high-speed internet connection. Ideally it will provide 10Mb download and upload speeds as a bare minimum. This will ensure that you aren't wasting time waiting for content to download and at the same time, that you are able to broadcast and watch video content. This is essential if for example, you want to host webinars without the quality of your output degrading for those who are watching. A quality, high speed connection is also necessary if you want to hold video-calls and meetings with others, online.

Here are some steps we recommend that will ensure that your connection is up to the job.

■ Check your connection speed regularly

You can test your speed at speedtest.net (they also have an app so that you can test your Wi-Fi using your phone).

It's worth testing your connection speed at different times of the day and night since these can vary depending on whether other people are connected or not. It may just reveal times of the day when your connection is slower.

If you don't have an uncontended line to your house, then your internet connection may be shared with others who are using the same provider in your neighbourhood. At the very least you may find that once other members of your household are home and using Wi-Fi that the quality of your connection drops off.

Testing the performance at various times may reveal the times of day when the connection is particularly strong and good for running webinars (for example). Other times may be better avoided, or you may have to kick other members of your household off the Internet if you need a dedicated connection!

■ Move your router closer to where you're working

Ideally the router will be located within your workspace such that you can enjoy a fast and stable connection to the Wi-Fi signal. While

Wi-Fi signals can be extended throughout homes using boosters plugged into the mains, some devices don't connect reliably to all models of booster.

Where possible, take Wi-Fi out of the equation. Even better is to plug your computer directly into your router with an ethernet cable if possible. Wired connections may seem a little 'old-school' but the speed and strength of connection will be consistent as a result of using a network cable to establish a hard-connection.

■ Speak with your service provider

It's certainly worth a call to your internet service provider to ask if your service can be improved or upgraded if necessary. It may be that they can offer you an updated router or move you to a higher performing service. But if neither of these are possible, you may need to move to another supplier if there is a better option in your local area.

You should also ask your provider if your internet plan has a data cap. Ideally you should be on an unlimited data plan as you don't want to run into limits at a crucial moment in a video call or a webinar!

■ Check who else is connected

It is worth checking out some Wi-Fi blocker apps to see what devices are on your Wi-Fi network at any given time. You can turn off Wi-Fi access for individual devices using these apps and this can be really useful for important online meetings where you need dedicated access. You may need to discuss this with household members though, as they may be affronted at you dominating the internet connection for your own needs!

A password-protected router will usually be effective and sufficient for restricting access to your internet connection. Many routers also have built in firewall software that prevents intrusions. But just occasionally you may find that others in the local area have managed to obtain your network key and are using your router without your permission. Password sharing on Apple iOS devices (for example) now makes it easier than ever to share network keys – either intentionally or inadvertently.

In order to preserve bandwidth for your own remoting needs, this is worth checking back on periodically too.

■ Other measures to improve connection speed

Here are a few other quick tips for things you can try to improve your connection speed. Some of these may help, if only a little bit:

1. Reset your router and modem on a periodic basis. You could use a timer plug to do this at night, automatically.

2. Install virus and malware scanners and run regular checks to see if there is anything nasty running on your computer that could be impacting on your internet connection speed, for example sending or receiving large packets of data back and forth across the internet for rogue purposes.

3. Clear your browser's cache on a regular basis. This can help to speed up your web browsing and it may well close down connections to websites that were running and updating themselves in the background.

4. Shutdown any unnecessary applications that are running in the background on your computer, as these may also be impacting on your access speed. Applications that share information in real-time (for example weather and location data, stock tickers and so-on) will be sending and receiving data for as

long as they are running, even if only in the background. It may even be worth checking which applications automatically start when you turn on your computer and turning them to manual instead.

■ Cyber Security

Whether you're remoting or not, having decent cyber security protection on all internet connected devices is essential these days. Don't assume that because you use a particular brand of device or a current version, that you are automatically protected.

Here are the basic guidelines:

1) Always install updates, patches and fixes to your software, apps and operating systems as soon as they come out.

2) Install a quality virus protection software package, update it regularly and carry out frequent scans – Kaspersky and McAfee produce industry-leading solutions.

3) Install and use a malware protection package – Malware Bytes is a good option.

4) On your smartphone, consider using a mobile app that protects your device and checks for rogue apps and data leakage (such as Lookout).

5) Use unique passwords on devices, websites and services and change them regularly.

6) Make use of password storage solutions such as Password Manager and Keychain on iOS devices.

7) Where websites and software services offer 2-Factor Authentication (where you get a passcode sent to your

smartphone at login), enable it and use it to prevent rogue logins.

8) Don't assume that because you are just one person, you aren't interesting to hackers!

These guidelines aren't intended to scare you, but given the degree to which we all rely on our computers and phones these days and the amount of data we generate in our daily lives, it makes sense to take all precautions possible. Protecting ourselves from cyber threats is a serious obligation that we all carry these days. Ignore it at your peril!

■ Your Computer

Just as internet speed is really important, so too is the speed of your computer. It can be easy to convince ourselves that we're saving money by not upgrading our computer regularly. The reality though is that a slow computer costs us time and money while we wait for it to catch up with us, whether that's for applications to open or for files to save or any other operation.

What's even worse is that using a poorly-performing computer can have a direct impact upon our health through the stress caused when it freezes for no apparent reason. This is especially so if we lose data or a complete document that we were working on when our computer crashed.

It can also be embarrassing to be that person on a video call whose connection keeps dropping or whose screen keeps freezing because they insist on using a low specification computer. It would be even worse in a scenario where you were trying to sell something online (for example, via a webinar) if your computer kept freezing during the presentation.

In recent years, computer chips, memory and storage have all benefited from rapid innovation – these all contribute to the speed of our computers making it sensible to consider upgrading regularly. To hold off doing so is a false-economy.

Investing in the appropriate technology, in the form of hardware, software and cybersecurity protection are all essentials for successful remoting.

■ Project Management

Whether our tasks are laid out for us by our employer or a supervisor, or we are responsible for determining our own priorities and organising our day-to-day action plan, project management is key to success.

You may think of project management as time management. In practice it may involve little more than making and maintaining a simple to-do list that prioritizes and tracks our workload and helps us to plan our work.

Getting organised about what you have to do and putting the tasks in some kind of logical order will do wonders for keeping you focused and maintaining productivity as you work remotely.

■ Goal Setting

A great place to start is to write out your goals, which will ideally align with your highest values, as previously discussed. The tasks that you prioritise at the top of your list would preferably be those that contribute most significantly to your goals. These, in turn will hopefully be aligned with your highest values.

A detailed exercise that guides you through the process of identifying and setting your long-term, medium-term and short-term goals is provided in the book RETHiNK Productivity – a companion book for RETHiNK Remoting. For more information, please follow the link below.

rethinkremoting.com

In *RETHiNK Productivity* we lead you through the process of identifying goals in each of the 8 core areas of your life, again using a different version of the RETHiNK acronym. In the case of goals, this is about considering and identifying your priorities in the following areas:

■ RELATIONSHIPS:

This is one of the easiest areas to understand and one of the most popular of all areas, the focus being on your family and immediate circle of friends. This begins with your immediate family unit of parents and children, as well as siblings and extended family. It reaches beyond family to include the friends you associate with the most. Since these are the people that you spend the most time with, they impact on your belief systems and earnings more than anyone else in your life.

■ EARNINGS:

This area is about your ability to earn money by exchanging your time for money. In essence, this means having a job, being self-employed or running a business where you are being paid directly in line with how many hours you work. It is the most common method for people to acquire money. The more experience you have and the more value you can provide to a company, generally the more you get paid per hour. The number of hours in the week that you work is your limiter in terms of earnings.

■ TAO:

Tao is a Chinese word that means the way, the path or the route. Tao is the underlying natural order of the universe. We use this word rather than "spirituality" because, firstly, there is no "S" in RETHiNK! But secondly, and more importantly, because the word "spirituality" is often placed in the same box as "religion", which has quite different meanings for individuals based on their background and upbringing. Tao may be as simple as a meditation or ritual practice.

HEALTH:

This is where you direct your attention to your physical body, your fitness, your interest in your appearance, your weight, your clothing, your exercise routines, your eating habits and anything else that's related to how you look and feel.

INVESTMENTS:

In this area, the main focus is specifically how money itself is used to earn more money. It focuses on how to save, grow, invest, compound and use money effectively. It also involves having a good understanding of the systems related to finances, such as the economy, and basically anything related to growing money without you having to exchange your time for money. In time, it allows you to become financially free.

NETWORKS:

This area is about the extended range of people you know or impact beyond your immediate set of "relationships" with family and closest friends. It is made up of your network of slightly more distant acquaintances, including former classmates, business connections, associates, work colleagues and, on a grander scale, the networks you can access to influence and impact locally, nationally and globally.

KNOWLEDGE:

This area is associated with your mental growth. It is about working on improving the grey matter between your ears. Growth of your knowledge can be achieved through traditional education, books, courses, coaching, mentoring and through dedicating time, effort and focus on pursuits of your specialised knowledge.

! FUN:

Although working on the other seven areas may be fun for you from time to time, it is much more reassuring to plan fun activities into your schedule, to ensure they happen. The use of a planner to set and track goals should not feel like a chore or as though you are living in a military boot camp! The goals and targets you choose will be inspiring to you. And you will use the fun area to plan in rewards and to ensure you make time to truly enjoy yourself.

Now that you understand each of the eight areas, you can shape what success might look like for you in each of them. To know what to prioritise and how to use your time effectively each day, you must first determine what you wish to achieve in each area.

RETHiNK Productivity contains a five-step exercise that helps you to identify and set goals for each of the RETHiNK! areas:

Step 1:
You will determine the goals you wish to achieve by the end of this year in each of the eight areas: Relationships, Earnings, Tao, Health, Investments, Networks, Knowledge and Fun!

Step 2:
Write each of them in "SMARTER" format: Specific, Measurable, Achievable, Relevant, Timebound, Evaluated and Reviewed. An example could be: *"I am exercising daily for a minimum of 15 minutes and have a resting heart rate of 55 bpm and body fat of 15% or less by 31st of December 2030 or sooner."* Do this on a blank piece of paper repeatedly until you arrive at the final wording you are happy with. This is what you'll enter into the *RETHiNK Planner* if you have one. If not, you can record your SMARTER goal somewhere else where you can refer to it often.

Step 3:
Once you are clear on your year-end goals in all eight areas, you then break them down into quarterly goals across the year. Make your best estimate of where you need to be at the end of each quarter to hit your year-end goals. You will get better at this every single quarter that you go through the planning process.

Step 4:
If you have a *RETHiNK Planner*, turn to the appropriate page for the current week and record your goals there. If you don't have a *RETHiNK Planner* yet, you can use a diary or notepad for now.

Step 5:

If you're using the *RETHiNK Planner*, it will lead you through a process of tracking and monitoring progress towards your goals.

For more detailed exploration of the goal-setting exercise, dive into the relevant sections of *RETHiNK Productivity* and *RETHiNK Time Management.*

If you are looking to make a quick start for now and don't have those books, you can still think about what you'd like to achieve in each of the RETHiNK! areas outlined above, and then break these down into some short-term goals to get started today.

rethinkremoting.com

- Prioritisation

With your short, medium and long-term goals set, you can now prepare and prioritise your action plan or to-do list. This will be made up of smaller, more granular tasks, the completion of which gradually accumulates to help you achieve your goals.

Small tasks feel much more achievable and less-daunting than one big task. The small achievements compound upon each other, building into big achievements.

A useful tactic for focus and to ensure you take regular breaks is to organise your tasks and your time using the Pomodoro method. We will look at this in more detail in the Healthzone chapter.

Writing or typing out your to-do list means you won't have to constantly use valuable brain power trying to remember all the things you want to get done in the course of a day.

The pleasure you'll feel and the sense of accomplishment that comes from crossing tasks off your list once completed will help to keep you going. It's also a good idea to reward yourself for positive achievements in order to keep yourself motivated.

Rewards could be something simple like merely acknowledging steps of progress to yourself - a virtual high-five or a pat-on-the-back. You may go further and treat yourself to something nice (that's in proportion to the scale of your achievement, hopefully!).

You could also colour in a printed progress bar for a visual representation of progress towards a goal.

If you find yourself caught up doing endless, repetitive tasks that don't feel like the best use of your time, and worse-still which do not move your closer to your goals then you should consider delegating them or hire a freelancer to complete them on your behalf. It's so easy these days to find and hire freelancers who charge a fraction of what you pay yourself to do these often-mind-numbing tasks, and which they actually enjoy doing.

▪ Where does the time go?

Another important tool for successful remoting is to make the clock work in your favour. Making the most of the time we have available is key to living a successful and fulfilled life.

It can be useful to go through an exercise periodically that helps you track the tasks and areas of your business or remote working that are taking up the majority of your time.

Having a better understanding of where your time goes will help you to re-design how you work (by eliminating some tasks and outsourcing others) so that you get maximum benefit from your time. Remember, time is the only truly finite resource and we cannot magically make more of it!

■ The three types of time

There are three different types of time, which are:

Unproductive time - time you spend not serving your goals.

Productive time - time you spend on your goals.

Super-productive time - time you spend training others and showing them how to serve your goals.

We would like to introduce you to one of our all-time favourite tactics for assessing where you are currently, in terms of how you spend your day and how optimally you use time. This was something we stumbled across and it's now one of the first recommendations we have for people who are serious about making best use of their time!

You cannot do this exercise until you have first drawn up a clear picture of what your goals are. The optimal use of time would be to make sure that as much of it as possible is super-productive, but before you can put a plan in place to make that so, you need to understand how you were spending your time before you were aware of these three types of time.

Completing the following exercise can be very revealing about your productivity levels! Here's how the exercise works.

Assuming that you start work at 9am, set your alarm clock for 9.10am. At 9.10 am, as soon as the alarm goes off, hit the snooze button and assess the work you were doing at the very second before the alarm went off. Was it unproductive, productive or super-productive?

Get three coloured markers in red, blue and green. Each time the alarm goes off and you press snooze, on an A4 sheet of paper take the appropriate marker and make a spot. Use red for unproductive, blue for productive and green for super-productive. After a few hours the sheet should begin to fill with dots. If you run out of space at the end of the page, start a new column and continue with the exercise.

There are some rules to the game (which we call a UPS check), to make it more impactful.

- **Rule 1:** While doing the exercise, you must have the sheet and three markers with you at all times, everywhere!

- **Rule 2:** You have to be honest and shouldn't overthink it. What you are doing is either aligned to your goals or not.

- **Rule 3:** Don't try to be more productive just because you are measuring it. This is an assessment of your current base state.

- **Rule 4:** Use it as soon as you wake until you sleep, ideally for five days.

- **Rule 5:** At the end of each day, add up how many of each of the dots there are and work out the percentage split of your time between Unproductive, Productive and Super-productive.

After day 1, review your results to reveal your base state. It may look something like this:

78% - Unproductive
16% - Productive
6% - Super-productive

The percentages above would indicate that the person in the study is doing a lot of unproductive tasks that could benefit from being outsourced to another person to do on their behalf. By outsourcing these tasks, you may find that repeating the check on another day starts to shift the balance to something more like this:

15% - Unproductive
50% - Productive
35% - Super-productive

If you do the UPS check often enough, you may start to find that you operate on auto-pilot.

What we have found is that just before the alarm goes off, people who are attuned to assessing their time begin to pre-empt the alarm and snooze it just as it's about to ring. After a week of conditioning, their brain starts doing an auto-UPS check on their productivity levels every ten minutes! Any time we find that our productivity levels are dropping off, this is the ONE thing that seems to bring them back up almost immediately.

We have received fantastic feedback on the power of this exercise over the past decade regarding the positive impact it has made to people's productivity levels.

In case you're in any doubt about how to reclassify different types of time, here are a few questions that often arise which may help add some clarity:

Q: When I am cooking dinner for the kids, is this productive time as having healthy children is one of my goals?

A: No. This is considered an unproductive task as it is a low priority. That task could be outsourced or replaced by having fresh organic meals delivered daily.

Q: *Is cleaning or shopping productive, as managing my family is a major goal?*

A: *No for the same reason as above.*

Q: *Is helping my children with their homework considered productive or super-productive?*

A: *Productive assuming that you couldn't have a tutor or one of your other children do it in your place.*

You may disagree with the answers above but it's our game and our rules! Here are some more examples of activities where you can make your time super-productive without showing someone else how to do tasks:

- Having dinner, but with people from whom you can learn, like mentors.

- Writing a book while away on holiday.

- Using social events as an opportunity to do some business networking.

- Making calls while travelling.

- Catching up on emails or meetings while on a train.

- Using flight time to think through higher level strategy (while keeping Wi-Fi off!)

- Listening to audiobooks or podcasts while exercising or driving.

Get into the habit of finding tasks that can be done at absolutely no extra cost to your time or focus.

By having a focus on making the majority of your time productive or super-productive, and by making sure that most of the things you work on are aligned to your goals and values, you will likely find that you get the best out of your remoting life.

If you're interested in using a tool for tracking your time, we also recommend the 'Toggl' app.

As you can now hopefully understand, successful remoting relies upon having access to, and using the appropriate tools in our daily working life, including:

- High speed, resilient internet access

- A highly performing computer with appropriate software and cybersecurity installed

- A useful set of project management and time management tools and habits – even if these are as simple as a structured to-do list and a technique for regularly checking that your time is being used productively.

Here are a few other tools that you might consider putting in place in due course. They're not as essential as the others, but these tools can serve a useful purpose in equipping us for success in our remoting ventures.

■ Other tools

Smartphone with an appropriate tariff – In the same way that a high-speed, reliable and resilient internet connection is an essential tool for remoting, similar attention should be given to your mobile phone. If you use your smartphone for business purposes, you should make sure that you have an appropriate tariff with as few limits on calls, texts and data-usage as possible. Many of the software and apps that we've discussed in this chapter also have versions for Apple and Android smartphones. Being able to do business while on the move is really useful if you spend your working life remoting. But this all starts with having a good contract that allows you to get on and do what you need to do, unimpeded. Consider upgrading your phone to a recent model too, as again, having an outdated model of phone can be a false-economy.

Backup tools for your computer – Businesses will usually ensure that all their core data and applications are backed up regularly to prevent loss or corruption of systems and data. If you're remoting and running your own business, you'll need to do this for yourself. A solid backup and recovery regime can be as simple as ensuring that you copy all of your essential files onto a remote hard-drive or USB memory stick on a weekly basis. If you get into the habit of copying all files at the same time each week, this will quickly become a routine. Consider keeping two weeks' worth of backups on a hard-drive, erasing the oldest one with your weekly backup. In the worst case, you'll only lose one week's worth of data. You could also use online storage for your data and files (such as Google Drive, iCloud or an application such as Dropbox).

A Safe or Strongbox – Once you've got a regular backup on a remote disk, you'll need somewhere safe to store it. Ideally this would be in a safe or strongbox, along with your other valuables. At a minimum though, you should keep your backup disk somewhere separate from your computer so that there's less chance of theft or damage of both of them through being in the same place!

One final thing we want to discuss in this chapter is how to set up a simple home studio.

■ Simple Studio Setup

Whether it's used for holding online meetings, for marketing purposes or for creating video content, being on camera has become an integral part of remote working.

This is especially relevant if your work or business involves teaching online, delivering live online workshops and webinars or selling your expertise online in the form of a video training course.

In order to present a professional appearance and to deliver the best quality content we can possibly create, it's really important that we do ourselves justice onscreen and it's a lot easier than you think. Here's what we recommend.

1. A High Definition webcam at eye level. For even better quality, you can use a DSLR or Mirrorless Camera.

2. 3 LED lights – 2 providing lighting from the front and one behind pointing at a plain wall. If you don't have a suitable plain wall you might consider setting up a nice clutter-free background. A bookshelf is a popular choice.

3. A good quality microphone that cannot be seen on camera, unless it's a clip-on.

An optional extra that we use often, is a green screen. This gives you a lot more flexibility when it comes to your background.

We've provided a complete list of the equipment that we use for video production. To get this list, please follow the link below.

■ Summing up

You should now have a good understanding of the tools that we recommend using within your remoting workspace.

In the next chapter- Healthzone - we will look at some proven techniques for taking care of your health while working remotely.

Healthzone

The letter 'H' in the RETHiNK Remoting Model stands for Healthzone.

Before we begin with this chapter, let us quickly repeat our disclaimer from earlier. In relation to all content contained within this book regarding matters of health, it is important to point out that neither of us are qualified medical doctors. Our content is provided for informational purposes only, and you are advised to consult your own doctor before making any changes in your lifestyle and habits that could affect your health and wellbeing. With that said, let's go!

Long before the pandemic employers recognised the importance of taking care of the wellbeing of their employees. This duty of care is about more than fulfilling a legal obligation that exists between an employer and their staff. Rather, it's about doing what's necessary to protect the mental and physical wellbeing of those that do the work so that they remain fit, well and able to work – for the long-term.

People who are healthy, comfortable and whose intrinsic human needs are taken care of in the workplace are more likely to feel able to give 100% effort to their work.

Measures to protect health and wellbeing at work could include a wide range of things, such as:

- Providing ergonomic, comfortable and well-maintained office furniture.

- Making sure the workplace is well lit and ventilated, and heated (or cooled) to an optimum temperature that suits most of the people present.

- Ensuring that the workplace is free from hazards and that employees are able to work safely without adverse effects on their health and wellbeing.

- Providing facilities to promote comfort – well-equipped toilets and washrooms, spaces to eat and drink, catering facilities, space for leisure and for meetings, places designated for religious worship and so-on.

- Encouraging staff to take regular breaks and taking steps to promote work-life balance.

The list could go on and on. If you've spent time working in one or more offices, you'll likely have seen the vast range of diverse facilities that different employers provide for their staff.

The bad news is that if you are going to spend the majority of your working life remoting, you'll need to make appropriate considerations and provide the necessary facilities and care for yourself.

The good news is that for the most part, you're only going to have to cater for your own needs and preferences!

■ Not to be taken for granted

Many of us are prone to taking our health for granted. As long as we feel okay, most tend to assume we're doing everything necessary to protect our health and wellbeing.

Unfortunately, we also tend to wait until something goes wrong – until we develop aches, pains or other symptoms before taking action. Very few do much (or enough) to proactively protect our health other than perhaps taking a few vitamins and getting a little exercise.

When it comes to remoting, it's easy to think that all it takes is to find a bit of space at the kitchen table or on the couch where you can plug in your laptop and pick up the Wi-Fi signal and you're up and running. Most who've worked remotely for any length of time though, will have learned the hard way that aches and pains can quickly develop from poor posture when we haven't set up our workstation properly.

The aches and pains that creep up on us – the sore shoulders, the back-aches, head-aches and strained eyes – develop slowly over time and are hard to recover from once we're suffering. The best cure to such conditions therefore, is prevention – from day one.

Without a facilities manager to set up our workspace and without occupational health professionals to care for our health and wellbeing at work, it falls to us to make sure we're set up for success. That goes for protecting our health as much as our productivity.

Giving the Healthzone adequate attention is about more than just setting up our workstation to maximize productivity and comfort. It's about taking a holistic approach to our health and wellbeing and being mindful of the many ways in which this could be influenced for the better or for the worse, by remoting.

Remoting can seem like an immediate step forwards in improving our work-life balance – but there are many ways in which the opposite can be true if we're not mindful of the shift that it really represents.

■ Be Present

Eleanor Roosevelt put it best:

"Tomorrow is a mystery. Today is a gift. That is why it is called the present."

One of the most significant ways in which things can go wrong if we let it, is that our work-life bleeds into our home-life. In the Environment chapter we touched on this and discussed the importance of separating work from our personal life.

In simple terms, we must remember to log out and switch off from work mode, just the same as we would if we were physically leaving an office building at the end of a work day.

For example, if you are a parent with young children, thinking about work when you are playing with them has 3 distinct disadvantages.

1. If your mind is elsewhere (i.e. thinking about work) then you are not fully present and so the time you're spending with them is less enjoyable. They may very well notice how distracted you are too, limiting the enjoyment they take from the time.

2. You won't get any meaningful work done by simply thinking about it while with your children, so the distraction isn't going to serve any useful purpose either.

3. When you do go back to work, you may end up thinking about and indeed regretting how you were not fully present when you were playing with your children. These feelings of guilt could well result in your work being of poor quality due to the distraction.

A vicious circle ensues.

The best antidote to this is to keep your life compartmentalised and to be present in whatever you're doing. When you're working, focus on doing your work to the best of your ability. When you're spending time with your kids, family, partner, friends or alone and doing something other than work – give your undivided attention to where you are and what you're doing.

Being present in this way, or at least having the intention to be present is a good guiding principle to ensure that you get the best out of yourself and from each aspect of your life.

▣ Sleep

The same process of distraction can apply when it comes to getting adequate, quality sleep. There is little that's worse than lying in bed thinking about work, regretting something that has happened or worrying about something you could have done or should have done. The same effects come about when we lay awake worrying about what we've got to do tomorrow.

When we should be relaxing or winding down into sleep, but instead we're awake and fretting, the net effect is we're not getting any sleep and not getting any work done either. We feel exhausted the next day as a result of having missed out on sleep, and often aren't as productive as we should be.

We suggest that if you cannot sleep, the best tactic is to simply remind yourself that you won't get any meaningful work done while lying awake and furthermore, you won't be very effective the next day if you are exhausted.

If you are struggling to switch off or to relax into sleep because your mind is racing, there are a few other things that you might try.

▣ Meditation and Mindfulness

Meditation isn't just a means of helping ourselves to relax and to reduce stress. It's also a performance-enhancer. It's one of the most powerful practices for getting in touch with our inner-self and for finding the bridge between our inner world and the outer world that we want to create.

It's an entry point into our future reality. It's the place from which we can create and make our wildest dreams come true. It's the stairway to manifesting our ideal life. As such, meditation plays an important part in reinventing ourselves!

There have been over 6,000 peer-reviewed scientific studies carried out on meditation. Jonathan Haidt, author of *'The Happiness Hypothesis'* describes meditation as a "magic pill" for reducing anxiety and maximising our contentment in life.

It's also a wonderful way to stimulate the parasympathetic nervous system and engage in a period of recovery. While some of the most powerful times to meditate are when you first wake up and when you go to bed, meditation can also be used as a post-lunch rejuvenator to power afternoon productivity.

Think of your brain as a computer. As you think different thoughts or do different things, it's as though you are opening new windows on your computer. After an hour or two, your computer is slower and less responsive since so much of the computing power is being used to run all those open windows and applications. This is essentially what is happening to our brain as we progress through each day.

Meditation is a means by which we can close down some of those applications that are using our brain's computing power and consuming our energy and focus. It gives us a tool to reduce the burden of stress and allows us to concentrate on the task at hand, or to relax into sleep.

There are many free and low-cost meditation apps that will guide you through a short, basic meditation, including Headspace, Calm, Waking Up and Insight Timer.

A basic meditative practice can include simply sitting quietly with your eyes closed, gently following the breath. When you notice yourself becoming distracted by thoughts, note that you'd become distracted and return to the breath.

We've found that 10-minutes of meditation each day can bring enormous benefits.

To learn more about different forms of meditation including Transcendental Meditation, and the Silva method, feel free to check out RETHiNK Health on how to practice the meditation techniques and to understand the science behind why they work.

You can also access valuable insight into matters of health and guidance on how to build helpful routines and incorporate healthy habits into your life, within RETHiNK Productivity.

Please follow the link below for more details.

rethinkremoting.com

■ Practising Gratitude

Another powerful way of minimizing stress and dissatisfaction, and of helping ourselves to relax and sleep when we want to, is to become more mindful and purposeful about practicing gratitude.

Gratitude is a way of appreciating what you have, instead of always reaching for something new in the hope that it will make you happier. Gratitude helps us to focus on what we have instead of what we don't have.

When you introduce a daily practice of conscious, mindful gratitude you will notice the positivity flow into your life, along with a greater amount of empathy and altruism.

In positive psychology research, gratitude is strongly and consistently associated with greater levels of happiness and health. It helps people feel more positive emotions, enjoy good experiences, enhance their health, deal with adversity and build strong relationships both at work and at home.

One simple way of practicing gratitude in your daily life is to build it into your journaling process. Journaling is the process of taking a few moments each day to write down your thoughts, ideas and reflections in a journal or diary. The journal is for your own purposes only, and what you write doesn't have to be structured, ordered or even coherent! The act of writing things down helps to quieten the mind and bring order to disparate thoughts and ideas that might otherwise feel confusing and overwhelming.

A gratitude practice could be as simple as bookending each day by recognizing three things each morning that you are grateful for. At the end of each day, note a further three things that went well and something that could have made the day even better too. This helps to set the tone for the day ahead, celebrates what you have achieved at the end of that day and encourages a positive outlook for the next day to come. More importantly you are training your brain to recognise the positives and the good things that have happened rather than focusing on the bad.

The *RETHiNK Planner* encourages you to recognize steps of progress that were made towards your goals, and incorporates a space for you to note down what you are most grateful for as you reflect on each day. You can find out more about the RETHiNK Planner via the link below.

rethinkremoting.com

You hopefully now appreciate some of the diverse practices that you can include in your daily remoting life, that will encourage and promote mental clarity and calm, as well as ensuring that you're able to wind-down, relax and sleep soundly at the end of each day.

Healthzone is as much about doing the right things for your physical health as it is about equipping yourself to thrive mentally. With this in mind, we'd like to recommend some more things that we believe are fundamental to your health and success, as you embrace remoting.

■ Get outside

It's enormously important to make sure that you get some fresh-air in the course of each day. Remoting can make it easy to get so immersed in our work without outside distractions and interruptions that we fail to make time for breaks or even to eat and drink.

Making time for these things is vitally important, as is making sure that we don't end up spending the entire day indoors from waking, through working and going to bed again, without stepping outside.

To address this, we recommend that you go outside in the early part of the day and get access to some natural sunlight. This is important for aligning your circadian rhythm which in turn helps you sleep at appropriate intervals.

Try to spend a minimum of 15 to 20 minutes outside in the early morning. This could involve drinking your morning cup of tea or coffee outside, doing some yoga or stretching or going for a walk. The main thing is to get outside and expose your skin to the natural daylight.

▪ Stand and Deliver

We've previously introduced the idea that sitting is the new smoking for the insidious effect that long periods of sitting can have upon our health. To counteract the adverse health risks presented by prolonged sitting, we strongly recommend standing for regular periods during the working day if this is an option for you.

There are a great range of sit-stand desks available for purchase, and these provide the flexibility to work at your computer while sitting or standing (or alternating between each). The proven health benefits of standing desks more than justifies the investment.

In our experience, standing regularly throughout the day and particularly during meetings and while recording videos really helps to sharpen focus. It also improves energy levels, helping to keep these in balance rather than cycling through peaks and troughs of energy and lethargy throughout the day.

Standing also helps us when delivering live training and presentations online. Standing in front of your camera often feels more like being there in the room with the course participants or audience. Feedback suggests that the effects are the same for the audience in that they feel better connected with presenters who are standing, and the audience thus-feels energised as a result.

■ Keep moving

Standing and moving also play an important role in ensuring that we don't gain weight or lose fitness and muscle tone as an unwanted side-effect of remoting.

If we spend too many of our daily waking hours sitting (whether that's working or in leisure) then we're unlikely to counterbalance the amount of food that most of us are used to eating, in the meals and snacks we consume each day. Moving regularly and keeping our metabolism primed and active is essential if we want to avoid putting on weight through moving less.

There's also a science-backed argument that an intense workout at the end of the working day isn't likely to offer as much benefit as we might think, when compared to low-impact, steady movement throughout the day.

In the book 'Boundless: Upgrade Your Brain, Optimise Your Body and Defy Aging' by Ben Greenfield, the author argues that a hard workout at the end of a day of sedentary activity results in an attempt to force blood through 'kinked' vessels". He explains that an intense workout at the beginning or end of the day is not even necessary-for or guaranteed to result-in weight loss. Instead, low level physical activity throughout the day is what's really needed.

Accepting the need to keep moving, here's how and why we recommend that you build movement into your working time.

The first step is to set a timer and get up and move every 15 to 20 minutes, while working and during breaks. You can use a Pomodoro app such as 'Focus Keeper' as your timer.

Joan Vernikos, advisor to NASA and author of *'Sitting Kills, Moving Heals: How Everyday Movement Will Prevent Pain, Illness & Early Death - & Exercise Alone Won't'*, says that being sedentary is like going out of your gravitational pull, something that actually ages you. After 20 minutes of inactivity, Vernikos says that your body starts to change in suboptimal ways.

Even if all you did was to stand up and shake out your body you would be benefiting it. For even better outcomes you may consider installing an under-desk treadmill or stationery bike so that you can walk or pedal while you work. If you are sitting for any length of time, set a timer for every 15 to 20 minutes to stand up and do some stretching or a quick burst of activity.

If a treadmill or stationery bike aren't practical, there are plenty of other exercises and activities that can be done with some basic equipment and a little space. Depending on your physical fitness and the space available to you, you may consider one or more of the following activities to do when your timer sounds:

- 10 to 15 burpees
- 60-seconds of mountain climbers
- 25 jumping jacks
- 15 to 20 kettlebell swings
- 2 minutes of rebounding on a mini-trampoline
- 60-seconds of skipping
- A couple of sets of TRX rows

For more information on how to build exercise and movement into your daily life, check out the appropriate sections in the book *RETHiNK Health* by following the link below.

rethinkremoting.com

■ Give yourself a break

It is extremely important to take regular breaks especially if you find yourself sitting and staring at a screen for long periods. Research shows that during prolonged periods of concentration while working at a computer screen, we tend to blink less which results in tired, dry eyes, temporary short-sightedness and a heightened risk of eye-strain and headaches.

Health and safety experts point to obligations in government guidelines for those who work with computer screens, to take regular short breaks away from the screen. Five or ten minutes each hour is generally recognised as adequate rest. Taking such rest can be encouraged and built into the structure of your work by using a methodology such as the Pomodoro technique. This is also great for encouraging focus.

This technique uses a timer to break work into intervals known as Pomodoros, which are usually 25 minutes in length, each separated by a 5-minute break. During the 25-minute period, you accept no interruptions. This time is for your key strategic activities, whatever your main money-making tasks, or tasks of greatest importance and impact may be.

At the end of the 25 minutes, you take a 5-minute break, during which you should stretch, walk around or go outside. It's also a good time to drink some water.

The free app that we recommend for practising the Pomodoro Technique is called 'Focus Keeper'.

■ Breath

It can be easy when we're working on something that requires deep concentration, to neglect our breathing. We're not likely to suffocate through forgetting to breath entirely of course, but it's easy to become so engrossed in our work that breathing becomes shallow and sporadic. This then interferes with our energy levels and may leave us feeling irritable, light-headed or lethargic.

To remedy this, we recommend using some of your 5-minute breaks to practice one of a number of breathing techniques that force us to breathe more deliberately and maximise the flow of oxygen into the body.

Here are a few techniques that you might like to try.

Box Breathing

This simple yet powerful breathing technique forces us to take slow, deep, deliberate breaths. It can heighten performance, clear the mind and improve focus while also being a powerful stress reliever that helps us to quieten the mind. It's commonly used by athletes, soldiers, police officers, and nurses. It helps to regulate the autonomic nervous system and calms us down.

To practice box breathing, simply breathe in for 4 seconds, hold for 4 seconds, breathe out for 4 seconds and then pause for 4 more seconds before repeating. Do this for a few cycles.

Long term improvements can arise in both heart rate variability and quality of sleep for those who practice box breathing on a regular basis. It's a great tool for clearing the mind.

4, 7, 8 Breathing

This involves breathing in through your nose for a count of 4, holding your breath for a count of 7 and then exhaling through your mouth more forcibly with a "whoosh" sound for the count of 8.

This should be repeated a minimum of 4 times to induce a state of relaxation. This style of breathing has been shown to increase the presence in the body of something called GABA (Gamma Aminobutyric Acid). This is an inhibitory neurotransmitter that is essential for the proper functioning of the brain and central nervous system. GABA has the effect of reducing excessive brain activity and promoting a state of calm.

You can learn about these, and other forms of breathwork and techniques for focusing and enhancing your breath – including Buteyko Breathing, Wim Hof Breathing and SOMA Breath by checking out the appropriate chapter in RETHiNK Health. Just follow the link below for more information.

rethinkremoting.com

A free app that we recommend for coaching breathwork is called 'Breathly'.

■ Routine and Working 9 to 5

An important aspect of maintaining work-life balance and caring for our health is in respecting the importance of routine. Modern technology means that our default setting is to always be connected and contactable. It makes the notion of working 9 to 5 seem almost laughable. It's a great song, but a flawed notion!

Working in an office environment we may have adopted the company's norms and built our routine around a standard working day. Such a routine may have set out (for example) what time we are expected to be in the office, what time we typically take breaks and for how long, when we have meetings and what time we go home or finish work.

With remoting we tend to be more responsible for setting and maintaining our routine and our working schedule. We may still need to be online during certain core hours so that we can connect with colleagues, business partners, clients and prospects during normal business hours. But remoting can help us to flex our working day to best suit our needs and preferences. Some may choose to start work early and finish correspondingly early too, while others will prefer to work later in the day.

It may be that we plan our work schedule so that we can accommodate the other commitments in our life, such as taking the children to school in the morning and collecting them in the afternoon. We may plan our day around exercise during lunchtime (for example).

The beauty of remoting is that we are likely to enjoy more autonomy in planning our time. The danger is that with no commute to bookend our day, that work expands to fill more and more of our time, if we lose the discipline of switching-off.

A great tactic to adopt here is to actually track your time, being sure to record when you start and finish work, take breaks and so-on. This ties in with the idea of project management mentioned earlier.

The act of logging time is a useful prompt to consider if we are actually doing enough, or more than is reasonably expected of us. It's a check to ensure that we're maintaining balance in our life.

The flexibility of being able to set our own schedule should be embraced as a positive side-effect of remoting. Use it to establish a routine that suits you, but which also lets you be there for those you care for as well. If you have a child, build their care into your schedule, for example by blocking out school pickup and drop-off. If you play sports or volunteer, schedule time to get work done before or after these activities.

Once you've set your schedule, make it visible to your co-workers, business partner and employees using a shared calendar. This way, they'll know when you're free to meet or contactable, and when you've blocked out work and personal times and aren't to be disturbed.

It's also a good idea to make sure friends and family understand your schedule and respect it. People who aren't familiar with the type of work you do may feel like you're just sitting there and that you can be interrupted or drop what you're doing on a whim. Of course, we know did that's not the case, particularly when working to a deadline.

Set boundaries and manage others' expectations by letting them know that working remotely doesn't mean you're free all the time. They shouldn't just call by unannounced because you're remoting, if that doesn't suit you!

■ Bookend your working day

Shutting off at the end of your working day, not just closing your computer, but also your 'working mind' is a powerful way to transition from work to relaxation time. To continue to perform at high levels and optimise our body and mind for success, we need to build in recovery cycles.

Our bodies and minds are not designed to be pushed and pushed until we eventually collapse into bed only to find that we can't sleep, or that we sleep initially but later find ourselves awake in the middle of the night thinking about the next day and our never-ending to do list.

To counter this unwelcome side-effect of being 'always-on', set a 'finish work time' at the start of each day and always aim to finish then or within 30 minutes of that time. This will ensure that you only focus on the highest value tasks and actually work for all the time that you are 'at' work.

At the end of your day, maybe spend a few minutes journaling on what you achieved, what your number one task is for the next day and what you learnt. These activities will free up mental space and help you to sleep better. This is the perfect time to complete the appropriate sections in your RETHiNK Planner.

rethinkremoting.com

■ Take a shower or bath to wind-down

We're not here to advise you on how to keep yourself clean, but when it comes to relaxing at the end of a working day and preparing yourself for a good sleep, either a cold shower or a warm shower or bath can help you to wind down.

For some people, a cold shower cools the body ready to relax in readiness for sleep. Others find that a warm shower or bath relaxes them ready for sleep, especially when combined with magnesium salts and/or essential oils.

Experiment to find what works most effectively for you. Using natural products containing essential oils such as lavender can also help to encourage better sleep.

■ Digital sunset

Ninety minutes before bed, we recommend that you stop using electronic devices or watching television. If this is not possible, wear a pair of blue-light blocking glasses. These are not all created equal, and quality matters. As such, avoid cheaper pairs which do not always block out sufficient amounts of blue light in order to make a material difference. This will help your brain to slow down in readiness for sleep.

■ Stop eating and drinking 3 hours before bed

To give yourself the best chances of sleep, stop eating and drinking at least three hours before bed. This will help to keep insulin levels low, lower your resting pulse, lower your body temperature and prepare the body for sleep.

For more information and suggestions on ways that you can

improve the quality and quantity of your sleep, check out the appropriate sections of RETHiNK Health:

rethinkremoting.com

■ Summing up

You hopefully now appreciate the importance of taking care of your health and adopting habits and practices that will help you to protect and promote your health and wellbeing. Giving these due consideration, and finding the things that work best for you are an essential part of looking after yourself. As with all things health-related, proactive and preventative measures are far better than having to fix problems that arise through bad habits.

Protect your health!

In the next chapter we're going to explore how to go about integrating all aspects of the RETHiNK model.

Integrate

The letter 'I' in the RETHiNK Remoting Model stands for Integrate.

As this point in the book, you will hopefully have noticed that the different parts of the model integrate closely with each other. Not only are they all important in their own right, but many of them are interdependent as well. Doing them all properly will maximise the benefits you can expect to experience in your remoting life.

This is also true for the final 2 parts of the model that follow this chapter - Network and Knowledge-base.

For the purposes of understanding the Integrate chapter, you can think of Network as being the people who we interact with throughout our lives. The Knowledge-base is the means by which we ensure we're always tapped into the latest ideas, technologies and opportunities to support us in our reinvention.

■ The RETHiNK Remoting model - greater than the sum of its parts

In this chapter we are going to look at how each part works together; helping you to build a solid structure for your remoting life with great habits that lead to great results and meaningful success, both from a career and personal standpoint.

Here's how the model integrates in practice.

The **R**einvent chapter highlighted how we can use remoting as the stimulus to reinvent our ourselves and to reboot our lives, reshaping what we do and how we do it.

That **R**einvention could involve us pursuing a program of education or learning new skills. It could be centred on us working on a project alongside our job, or starting a new business. It might mean embarking on a process of personal growth and development to become a better version of who we were yesterday. The depth and extent of our **R**einvention will vary from person to person.

That process of **R**einvention doesn't happen by sheer will alone though. It comes about when we establish a well-equipped working **E**nvironment that stimulates and supports us to produce our best work. Within that **E**nvironment we will have access to the most useful and appropriate **T**ools that allow us to do our work to the best of our ability.

The right combination of **E**nvironment and **T**ools helps us to be productive, but it also impacts positively on our **H**ealth, too. If we have taken the appropriate steps to prioritise measures that promote our mental and physical health, we'll feel energised and enthused as we do the work necessary to **R**einvent ourselves.

Our working **E**nvironment, the **T**ools we use, the measures we adopt to promote our **H**ealth and the **N**etwork of people that we nurture, maintain and develop, all contribute to our sense of wellbeing. They help us maintain our work-life balance and ensure that we are enjoying the personal-interactions that every human needs to enjoy, to feel a sense of community and purpose.

The **K**nowledge-base that we are connected to, helps us keep up to date with new and exciting ideas, technologies and ways of working remotely so that we can continue our **R**einvention, whether that's building a business or continuing to learn.

You can hopefully now understand why each element of the model is important. That's not to say that you can't expect results if you are only able to cater for certain aspects of the model. But you'll get the best results if you give each of them due consideration.

- If the Environment aspect of RETHiNK Remoting is a challenge and you are struggling for space at home, it doesn't mean you're doomed to failure. If you don't have a spare room and have to compromise by sharing space with others in your household then you can still successfully work remotely. It might just take a little more consideration and patience towards and from other members of your household than if there's a dedicated space that you can call your own.

- As a result of the global pandemic we've all had to compromise on not being able to Network and meet up in person with others as much as we might like. It demonstrated to many, just how valuable it is to be able to meet others in person, even if that's just for a coffee and a chat. But it also taught us that there are alternative ways of getting together, whether for work or for fun using online meetings and webcams. If Network is your area of greatest challenge, because you live a long way away from those you work or do business with, remoting can still be made to work successfully, by exploiting the tools for remoting.

- If you're not able to invest in all the facilities and technologies that can boost your chances of success, it doesn't prevent you from making the best of the tools that you have available to you. These days, with a laptop and an internet connection there is very little that cannot be achieved when it comes to knowledge work. Certainly, a higher-powered laptop and high-speed fibre internet connection are preferable, and a green-screen and lighting can help you make videos that are more professional-looking. But if you have to make do with what you have, or what you can afford, using free versions of software and so-on then you can still be successful.

■ Summing up

Our point is that while all aspects of the RETHiNK model are important and beneficial, don't be deterred from reinventing yourself via remoting just because you think it will be too complex or costly to put it all in place, or because you don't have the time and resources to address all the elements of the model at once.

Now it's time to look at Network in more detail.

Network

n this chapter, we are going to look at the N in the RETHiNK Remoting Model which stands for Network.

■ Lonely and isolated

Some people find that working on their own for the majority of the time can make for quite a lonely existence. Remoting or working alone in any setting can be quite isolating and daunting for those who rely on social contact. Given the amount of time we spend in work, it's often the place where friendships and even relationships are forged, and without such social contact, many end up feeling isolated.

It's something of an irony that we don't usually choose who we work with, particularly when we work for larger businesses. And yet, we're thrown into working environments where we spend a lot of time with those people and as such it's little surprise that many friendships and even relationships are forged at work.

When we shift to remoting, that regular social contact and personal interaction can be immediately lost. It's important not to become a recluse and to feel perpetually isolated from others.

There's a balance to be struck then – between embracing remoting for all the possibilities it provides for reinventing ourselves, while still ensuring that we get enough contact and social interaction with others to make us feel part of a collective society.

■ Free from distractions

Other people prefer flying solo and have no problem at all with spending the majority of their working time alone. For such people, working in close proximity to others seems mostly to result in regular distractions and interruptions. In an office environment people are more likely to stop by your office or desk for a chat – whether related to work or not. While social contact is important, for some it can be a distraction that interrupts flow and becomes annoying.

The background noise and the hustle-and-bustle of an office can be comforting to some, but others may prefer to work in silence or with background noise of their own choosing – for example, music of a particular style or genre. Some may like working with the window open and a steady flow of fresh air, but this can often be a problem in an office where co-workers complain of feeling cold.

Remoting gives you the freedom to adjust the parameters of your working environment to suit your own tastes. If you want the window open in the depths of winter, and heavy metal music playing in the background to help you concentrate, then so be it. As we've already discussed, this is a real positive – but it can come at the expense of having a network of other people around you.

■ Does remoting inhibit innovation?

Employers that object to remoting and want to justify bringing their workforce together in a conventional office setting will often point to the spontaneous generation of ideas and the collective troubleshooting that they believe only happens when people spend time in close-proximity to their co-workers. Their argument tends to follow that creative and innovative ideas are often the product of spontaneous conversations and of kicking around ideas in informal conversations that can only occur when teams are co-located in an office.

This may be somewhat true, but it's not quite so black and white as some managers make out.

There's something to be said from being able to talk through problems or discuss ideas with co-workers, spontaneously as they come up. That said, online collaborative working tools and communication platforms now include virtual whiteboards, instant messaging facilities and encourage voice and video conferencing. As such, there's really little barrier to these sessions being held remotely instead of in person. Indeed, many teams these days are distributed around the globe and so face-to-face in-person sessions aren't even feasible.

Being together in one place with co-workers or business partners isn't a prerequisite for solving problems and generating good ideas. Remoting may require that more emphasis is placed upon scheduling regular catch-ups where teams kick around ideas rather than following a set agenda. It may also require that teams are encouraged to reach out and communicate with each other as needed, spontaneously, whilst also respecting each other's time.

■ Balance in all things

In our experience, there's a good case to be made for balance. Having some interaction with other people during the working day is usually a good thing, even if it's not a part of every working day.

Interacting with others, whether via a video call, an online chat, a phone call or even meeting up for a coffee can be a good way of making sure that you don't become isolated or too inwardly-focussed. Another option for building social interaction into your life could be to organise or participate in a social event like an online table quiz using a tool like Kahoot.

Bear in mind too, that social interactions in-person will yield benefits for mental health. As such, Network integrates with the Healthzone!

Whether you think of it as simply maintaining friendships or keeping in touch with co-workers, we like to think of this as part of the networking that underpins all successful businesses.

How we network can take many forms, ranging from company meetings or conferences if you work for an organisation, through to short online chats with friends or colleagues.

Working from home might seem like a solo experience, but it usually still involves interacting with others, whether it's meeting with your team, being given assignments, making decisions, or giving and receiving feedback. For this reason, it's important to establish and embed methods for collaboration while you work remotely.

■ Co-working hubs

Since the global pandemic, many companies have realised that they don't need to maintain as much permanent and dedicated office space for their staff. In some cases, this is resulting in office space being closed or repurposed. Other companies are taking the opportunity to diversify and change their offices into commercial co-working hubs where various companies co-locate to make more efficient use of the space.

Even before the pandemic, many firms offered serviced office accommodation within co-working hubs. In such locations, remote workers are able to access the basic resources that all knowledge workers require – a desk and office chair, high speed internet access and perhaps some basic IT peripherals (such as a computer monitor and keyboard to connect to their own laptop).

For payment of a fee, be that by the hour or day, or for a longer-term contract, knowledge workers are able to use the facilities and do their work remotely, but while surrounded by others doing similar work.

This seems like a good alternative to remoting completely alone, for at least part of the time. It allows personal contact with others but may result in less interruptions and distractions.

In a co-working space, the watercooler meetings can also be a nice way to take a break and meet new people. It often seems to turn out that such conversations can lead to business opportunities or prompt ideas for collaboration. It's not who you know but who knows you - you never know who you might connect with as a result of these spontaneous conversations.

■ Summing up

You hopefully now understand the importance of Network in successful remoting. Interpersonal contact shouldn't just be about formally scheduled meetings, whether in-person or held remotely using voice or video conference. It can also come about through informal and spontaneous catch-ups whether online or in person, meeting up with friends or business associates for a coffee, or simply from picking up the phone and reaching out to someone for a chat.

And if you get too lonely remoting from home, we recommend that you look into a co-working space to provide a little more of the hustle and bustle of the office environment.

We're now going to move onto the final element of the RETHiNK model.

Knowledge-base

A s we reach the last element of the RETHiNK model, where K stands for Knowledge-base, you're hopefully keen to get started on your remoting journey.

One thing to bear in mind as you do so, is that the world is constantly changing and technology continually evolving with it. If your ways of working were altered by the onset of the global pandemic, then you may have been forced to work from home where previously you were going into an office every day.

Companies quickly had to adopt tools that supported remote working, in the same way that many of us started to use technologies like Microsoft Teams and Zoom, to hold virtual face-to-face get-togethers with friends and family.

This period of rapid and unprecedented change was forced upon us by the pandemic, but it demonstrated how rapidly our situations can change and how technology providers quickly develop, enhance and scale their solutions to meet the needs of the world. What's also striking is how quickly many of us adapted-to and accepted this as a new normal.

Accepting that technological innovation will continue, it's of paramount importance to keep yourself up-to-date with current trends and developments that will make your life easier and more successful.

That's where the Knowledge-base comes in. It is through the Knowledge-base that we can remain in touch with you and bring periodic updates regarding services, tools, technologies and business opportunities that may be of use or interest to you.

If you want to stay in touch with us and receive periodic updates and invites to webinars and events that we believe may be interesting, consider joining our network by following the link below.

Furthermore, if you're

- interested in maximising your personal productivity and effectiveness

- keen to take a deep-dive into how to make best use of your time and techniques for managing it

- familiar with the RETHiNK Planner and want to order further copies of it to record and monitor progress towards your goals

- focused on how to create, market and sell your own training courses to market and monetise your skills and expertise

- interested in social media marketing as a route to your new online business

- keen to understand the many ways in which you can promote and take care of your health and wellbeing

then follow the link below.

rethinkremoting.com

What next?

Well, we've reached the end of RETHiNK Remoting. Hopefully by now you're excited to begin your remoting journey and itching to get started with reinventing yourself. You may even have already begun!

If you're hesitant about anything, or doubt that you'll be able to adapt to this exciting and revolutionary new way of working (and living), there is no substitute for getting started – NOW!

If it seems daunting, the best thing to do is to just get started. You hopefully appreciate that successful remoting is about more than just connecting your laptop to your Wi-Fi, sitting at your kitchen table and logging on – but that's a good place to start! Everything else can be built upon that.

Here's a final reminder of the RETHiNK remoting model:

R - REINVENT

E - ENVIRONMENT

T - TOOLS

H - HEALTHZONE

I - INTEGRATE

N - NETWORK

K - KNOWLEDGE-BASE

We wish you well with your reinvention and hope that you're able to take full advantage of the remoting revolution!

All the best,
Paul O'Mahony and Johnny Beirne

Notes

Made in the USA
Las Vegas, NV
11 December 2021

37156680R00066